Bottom Fishing fo
Willing to Take Ridiculous Cases

HOW TO HOOK A SHYSTER

Kenneth L. McElwee

Piquant Publications, L.L.C.

Piquant Publications, L.L.C.
Books That Hook
E-mail: info@BooksThatHook.com
Copyright ©2011, Kenneth L. McElwee
All rights reserved.

ISBN-10 0-9830246-0-X
ISBN-13 978-0-9830246-0-6
Library of Congress Control Number: 2010917265
Copyright information available upon request.

Cover Design: Mary Fisher Design
Interior Design: J. L. Saloff, Saloff Enterprises

v. 1.0
First Edition, 2011
Printed on acid-free paper.

**This work is composed of a series of correspondence from a fictitious person, J. Morgan Dumont, III, to real lawyers. However, the actual names of the replying attorneys, their law firms, partners, associates and counsel have been changed. Moreover, the contact information as well as the signatures of lawyers responding to Mr. Dumont's letters have been redacted. Any resemblance between the changed names of responding lawyers, their law firms and associated personnel is coincidental only. Although the letters authored by the fictitious Mr. Dumont cite some real events, facts and places in order to advance each letter's storyline, Mr. Dumont's narratives are fabricated and any resemblance to actual persons or entities is purely coincidental.

DEDICATION:

No one, but no one,

wants me to dedicate this book to him.

A special Scotsman's thanks to:

J. L. Saloff, who, with a mystical touch, skillfully tightened the nuts and bolts of my pedestrian project without ever screwing me financially!

And to:

Mary Fisher, who expertly baited my book's hook with an irresistible cover design without gaffing me monetarily!

CONFIDENTIAL

CONTENTS

CHAPTER 1

Mr. Dumont's Tax Loophole

J. MORGAN DUMONT, III

POST OFFICE BOX 266
HOLICONG, PENNSYLVANIA 18901

January 28, 2009

Maryanne M. Williams, Esq.
██████████████████████

Suite ██████   CONFIDENTIAL
Philadelphia, Pennsylvania 19107

Dear Ms. Williams:

I am in need of a lawyer, and a mutual acquaintance has recommended that I contact you. I am prepared to pay a non-refundable flat fee of $100,000 to the lawyer who I select to help me in a plan that I have devised to legally avoid (not evade) the payment of federal inheritance tax upon the death of my widowed mother. (I don't like paying lawyers by the hour because it encourages inefficiency and waste.) Although I realize that sophisticated legal advice often costs more than $100,000, I thought that you might nevertheless be tempted to assist me if I paid a flat fee up front.

My mother, who is presently 88 years old, is a very wealthy woman. Her liquid assets alone exceed $80,000,000, and her estates in Palm Springs, Lake Lucerne Switzerland, and Nice, France, (not to mention her East Side triplex) are worth many, many millions. I realize that upon my mother's death, her estate will be subject to federal inheritance tax at above the 50% bracket. This tax is grotesquely confiscatory, and I have done some research of my own in order to avoid that result.

I understand that if (1) my father were still alive and (2) my mother then predeceased him, her entire estate would have passed to him tax free pursuant to the federal marital exemption for inheritance tax. I also understand that on the Island of Truk in the South Pacific, statutes protecting native religion allow the continuation of a fertility ceremony in which a widowed mother may marry her son. Truk is an autonomous state and its family laws are recognized and upheld as binding by the United States pursuant to a post-World War II treaty. I have already made arrangements with the authorities of Truk to conduct the marriage.

My plan is this: My mother and I will fly to the Island of Truk and get married, and we will have a marriage certificate issued to us. I understand that because my marriage on Truk would be recognized by U.S. treaty, I cannot be prosecuted under U.S. law. The obvious point of this exercise is to avoid the confiscation of millions of dollars of my mother's property upon her passing.

My immediate problem is this: I understand that, pursuant to common law principles, a marriage can be declared a nullity in many states if it was never consummated. I am concerned that the government might raise this issue after my mother's demise in order to invalidate our union and thereby tax my mother's estate. Accordingly, the question that I need to be addressed is whether I must consummate my marriage with my mother in order to preempt such an anticipated argument by the government. Given the amount of money involved, I would normally just do it, but since my mother is 88 years of age, I'm concerned that our wedding night might be physically exhausting and (perhaps) fatal for her.

Are carnal relations really necessary in order to make our marriage unassailable by the federal government? Do you see any other issues that I might have overlooked? Please note that my plan is irrevocably set. Accordingly, if you identify problems with my plan, please don't stop there—offer solutions. I am interviewing one other lawyer, and I am asking both of you to give me your preliminary thoughts in writing on this issue. I will review and compare your replies in determining which lawyer should be retained. Kindly correspond with me promptly.

Very truly yours,

J. Morgan Dumont

J. Morgan Dumont

JMD/km

LAW OFFICE OF
MARYANNE M. WILLIAMS, ESQUIRE

*Helping to Put
Your Legal House
In Order.*

February 2, 2009

Mr. J. Morgan Dumont, III
P.O. Box 266
Holicong, Pennsylvania 18928-0266

Dear Mr. Dumont:

I am writing this letter in response to your letter of January 28, 2009. While your letter was interesting and detailed, it did not contain enough information for me to decide whether or not I will be able to take your case. At the same time, I would like to provide you with some answers to questions you raised in your letter.

First of all, in the Commonwealth of Pennsylvania, if a marriage is not consummated, only the parties to the marriage can contest it, not any third party. This means that a marriage does not have to be consummated to be valid. However, under Pennsylvania law, marriages between mothers and sons are void and thus will not be recognized by the Commonwealth of Pennsylvania. I believe this will be the case in most states as well.

Secondly, I am curious as to why you have not explored trust options including living trusts and things of that nature rather than a marriage with your mother. Marriage with your mother and having carnal relations with your mother seems a quite drastic and unneeded means of avoiding inheritance taxes.

If you would like to explore other options for legally avoiding inheritance taxes to the full extent permitted, please contact me so that we can explore these options and devise an alternate plan involving gifts, trusts, and similar options.

Additionally, it would be greatly appreciated if you would let me know who referred you to my office. My business grows only due to referrals from kind and satisfied clients and I would like to be able to send a thank you note to the person who referred you.

Philadelphia, Pennsylvania 19107
phone (215)
fax (215)

LAW OFFICE OF
MARYANNE M. WILLIAMS, ESQUIRE

Once again, thank you for the opportunity to be of service and best wishes in the future.

Sincerely yours,

*Helping to Put
Your Legal House
In Order.*

Maryanne M. Williams, Esquire
Attorney-at-Law

Great!!
Hire this Lawyer!!

Philadelphia, Pennsylvania 19107
phone (215)
fax (215)

J. MORGAN DUMONT, III

POST OFFICE BOX 266
HOLICONG, PENNSYLVANIA 18901

February 9, 2009

Maryanne M. Williams, Esq.

██████████████████████

Suite,████████   CONFIDENTIAL
Philadelphia, Pennsylvania 19107

Dear Ms. Williams:

Thank you for your thoughtful reply letter of February 2, 2009. Mother and I would like to meet with you. To that end, we'll drop in at your office on February 24, 2009, at 11:00 A.M. We will bring our relevant financial documents to the meeting. Unless that time is inconvenient for you, we'll see you then.

In your letter, you raised several issues that I want to address.

First, I did not pursue a trust mechanism because Mother wants me to have the money outright so that I will have unfettered use of the entire sum. If Mother's estate were left in trust, unacceptable restrictions would be placed on me.

Second, I think you might be mistaken about your conclusion that my marriage to Mother would be held to be void under Pennsylvania law. I'm no lawyer, but I do know a little about the Constitution. Under both a United States Treaty and a federal statute, Truk's family laws are recognized as binding. I remember reading about the Supremacy Clause in college and how federal law effectively trumps any contradictory state law. In other words, I don't think that the Commonwealth of Pennsylvania may nullify a marriage that has been blessed by Uncle Sam. What do you think?

Third, I want to address the issue of consummating my union with Mother. I appreciate your point that only spouses may contest a marriage by arguing that it was never consummated. Nevertheless, I still think that our coupling is necessary. After all, suppose Mother decides to change her mind about our marriage after the ceremony and tries to divorce me? If we make love on our wedding night, she won't be able to use that argument against me.

One issue that neither of us has addressed occurred to me yesterday. As you know, Mother, who turned 89 last week, has a heart condition. I always assumed that consensual carnal knowledge between spouses is absolutely privileged and inviolate. However, I'm concerned that I might have some type of criminal culpability if sex with Mother proves fatal. Please advise.

In any event, I look forward to meeting you.

Very truly yours,

J. Morgan Dumont

LAW OFFICE OF
MARYANNE M. WILLIAMS, ESQUIRE

*Helping to Put
Your Legal House
In Order.*

February 16, 2009

J. Morgan Dumont, III
P. O. Box 266
Holicong, Pennsylvania 18928-0266

Dear Mr. Dumont:

Unfortunately, I will be unavailable to meet with you on February 24 since I have scheduled commitments for that day. It will be necessary for you to call my office to arrange an appointment. At that appointment, it will be appropriate for us to enter into a formal retainer agreement if you wish me to proceed with your matter. Therefore, I am enclosing a retainer agreement along the lines of what you first proposed in your letter of January 28, 2009. Kindly review it in advance of our meeting. Thank you.

Please bring whatever documents you have that you believe are relevant to your tax planning issue concerning your mother's estate. Although I will be prepared to discuss your plan to avoid the imposition of inheritance tax upon your mother's passing, I intend to review your matter fresh and will advise you on what I believe to be the best overall tax strategy. In the meantime, I urge you not to go forward with your plans to marry and cohabitate with your mother pending the finalization of my review of your matter.

Sincerely yours,

Philadelphia, Pennsylvania 19107
phone (215)
fax (215)

Maryanne M. Williams, Esquire
Attorney-at-Law

MMW/ib

J. MORGAN DUMONT, III

**POST OFFICE BOX 266
HOLICONG, PENNSYLVANIA 18901**

February 23, 2009

Maryanne M. Williams, Esq.

███████████████████████

Suite ███████

Philadelphia, Pennsylvania 19107

CONFIDENTIAL

Dear Ms. Williams:

I was delighted to read that you need more time to review the matter afresh in order to decide whether or not my plan to marry Mother and "cohabitate" with her will successfully thwart the imposition of the our nation's confiscatory inheritance tax. You're obviously a very careful lawyer, and I like that. However, how long do you think it will take for you to draw your conclusion as to the legal propriety of consummating my union with Mother? We're making plans for our ceremony on Truk, and everyone from the caterers to the holy man we've hired are pushing us to commit to a date certain.

Mother feels a little awkward about the native ceremony that we've planned, especially because she'll be surrounded by primitives whose customs are decidedly different. Accordingly, Mother and I have decided that we would like to retain you for an additional service: We would be honored if you would accompany us on our private jet to Truk and stand beside Mother at the ceremony as a bride's maid. Of course, we'll pay you handsomely for your time as well as provide a luxurious, tropical bungalow next to the one that Mother and I will be using for our nuptials. And you can bring a guest! In anticipation of your acceptance of this honor (and of a free tropical holiday), we thank you from the bottom of our hearts.

The holy man we've hired insists on performing a traditional, native ceremony. It includes an exotic fertility dance between a native couple, which Mother and I feel is a bit silly in our case since she's decades past her child-bearing years. In any event, in keeping with Truk tradition, the female participants in the wedding must wear grass skirts and leis (and only leis) above. Luckily, the holy man has made an exception for Mother and her bride's maids who may wear strings of leis sewn onto a flesh-colored bodysuit. Accordingly, when we meet, you'll have to provide me with your clothing sizes for the grass skirt and bodysuit.

Unless it is inconvenient for you, Mother and I will be dropping in your office on Thursday, March 9, 2009, for our consultation. We can't wait to meet you.

Very truly yours,

J. Morgan Dumont

JMD/km

LAW OFFICE OF
MARYANNE M. WILLIAMS, ESQUIRE

February 28, 2009

Mr. J. Morgan Dumont, III
P.O. Box 266
Holicong, Pennsylvania 18928-0266

Helping to Put
Your Legal House
In Order.

Dear Mr. Dumont:

I have received your letter of February 23rd. It occurred to me that in dealing with your matter, we're putting the proverbial "cart before the horse". Instead of first researching the legal efficacy of your proposed strategy from a taxation point of view, it makes more sense for you to obtain first a legal opinion about the criminal consequences, if any, of marrying your mother.

If an experienced criminal attorney concurs that the United States and the Commonwealth of Pennsylvania are obligated to give full force and effect to Truk laws, including those sanctioning unions between sons and widowed mothers, then I will proceed with my tax analysis, including alternative estate planning strategies that I hope you will consider. I suggest that you consult a criminal attorney before meeting with me on March 9, 2009, as you have proposed. I have listed two below:

Frederick Driessen, Esq.   Jacob Mandelbaum, Esq.

█████████████████████   █████████████████████
█████████████████████   █████████████████████
██████████████   ███Suite ████████████
Philadelphia, PA 19103   Philadelphia, PA 19107
Tel. (215)███████████   Tel. (215)███████████

████████████████████
████████████████████
Philadelphia, Pennsylvania 19107
phone (215)████████
fax (215)███████

In conclusion, I want to thank your mother for the honor of being asked to serve as her bride's maid. Although I am flattered, my duties to my family and clients prevent me spending so much time away from my office, and I must, unfortunately, decline your gracious invitation.

LAW OFFICE OF
MARYANNE M. WILLIAMS, ESQUIRE

After you obtain an opinion from a criminal attorney, please telephone my office to schedule an appointment.

Sincerely yours,

*Helping to Put
Your Legal House
In Order.*

Maryanne M. Williams, Esquire
Attorney-at-Law

MMW/ib

Philadelphia, Pennsylvania 19107
phone (215)
fax (215)

J. MORGAN DUMONT, III

POST OFFICE BOX 266
HOLICONG, PENNSYLVANIA 18901

March 6, 2009

Maryanne M. Williams, Esq.

~~██████████████████~~

Suite ██████
Philadelphia, Pennsylvania 19107

CONFIDENTIAL

Dear Ms. Williams:

Thank you so much for your letter of February 28. I took your advice, and I retained a criminal attorney, although he was not one of the lawyers who you had recommended. He says he runs a "full service" law firm that can take care of my estate planning, tax and potential criminal matters. However, he's considerably more expensive than you—he demanded a non-refundable fixed fee of $250,000, but he was enthusiastic about helping me, so I paid him. I think it makes more sense for me to stick with one lawyer rather than to bounce from one firm to another.

By the way, there's one area of law that my new lawyer and his partners don't touch--parking ticket litigation. When I parked my Rolls in front of his office, a "lady" cop gave me a ticket because the meter had allegedly expired. (In fact, it expired just as I was getting into my car, but that bitch ticketed me anyway.) I'm outraged. This is a matter of principle to me, not money, and I'm willing to compensate you with an amount equal to the entire cost of the parking fine (regardless of whether or not you prevail in court) if you agree to represent me. Please advise.

Very truly yours,

J. Morgan Dumont

J. Morgan Dumont

JMD/km

NO REPLY!

Linda S. Jefferson
PO Box ████
████, FL ████

January 14, 2009

J. Morgan Dumont III
6901 W. Okeechobee Blvd., D-5
West Palm beach, FL 33411

Dear Mr. Dumont:

Just playing hard to get
Follow up letter Required

This is in response to your letter dated January 7, 2009, in which you request legal advice regarding your "irrevocable" plan. I must admit that the fixed fee you propose is enticing. However, there is one reason why I must decline to participate in your selection process.

I would decline because I would not be able to offer you the vigorous advocacy that every client deserves. I have no affinity for the tax system and have often counseled clients in ways they might reduce (i.e. lifetime gifts, charitable trusts, etc.) and/or postpone (joint tenancy with rights of survivorship) the taxation of their estate. However, your proposed solution is one which I find myself unable to defend and, in fact, is one my personal value system strongly opposes.

Your letter does not state certain material facts: (1) whether you are the sole heir at law of your mother; (2) whether your mother is legally competent; (3) whether you object to only inheritance tax or gift and income tax as well; (4) whether you have' consulted with a CPA regarding the tax implications of other alternatives; (5) whether your parents have some type of estate plan (i.e. a trust) already in place; and (6) who the "mutual acquaintance" is who recommended that I contact me.

There is no other attorney who I can proffer as a substitute candidate for myself. I request that you inform our "mutual acquaintance" that, despite my financial needs, I am disappointed that anyone who truly knows me would imagine that I would be able to put aside my personal moral and ethical position to the extent that your case apparently would require. I regret any personal insult my response might stimulate, but it is my belief that you are likely someone who is likely impervious to public opinion of himself.

Sincerely,

Linda s. Jefferson

J. MORGAN DUMONT, III

6901 W. OKEECHOBEE BLVD., D-5, BOX 161
WEST PALM BEACH, FLORIDA 33411

February 11, 2009

Linda S. Jefferson, Esq.
P.O. Box ▮▮▮▮
▮▮▮▮▮▮▮▮, Florida ▮▮▮▮▮

CONFIDENTIAL

Dear Ms. Jefferson:

I have distributed your reply correspondence to my new friends on Truk. Every native who read your letter was offended by it. Matrimony between widowed mothers and their sons is a sacred rite among my adopted people. Your hostile condemnation of that rite — a rite that is both recognized and upheld as legal pursuant to United States treaty--belies your prejudices and evidences your own sexual hang-ups.

Mother and I are proud to have registered as citizens of Truk and to have adopted its ways. I trust that, with this explanation, you will reconsider your position.

Mother and I will be in your neck of the woods in the coming weeks. (The seamstress who we've hired for her wedding gown lives close by). Unless I hear from you to the contrary, Mother and I will drop in on February 24, 2009, at 3:00 P.M.

Trusting that your previous correspondence is now "water under the bridge," Mother and I both look forward to meeting you.

Very truly yours,

J. Morgan Dumont

J. Morgan Dumont

Linda S. Jefferson
PO Box
█████, FL ██████

PRIORITY MAIL

February 17, 2009
J. Morgan Dumont III
6901 W. Okeechobee Blvd., D-5
West Palm Beach, FL 33411

Dear Mr. Dumont:

I assume our "mutual acquaintance" has also told you where I have my home office since my street address does not appear on my letterhead. You are a seriously disturbed person. Under no circumstances come to my home. You will not be received on February 24, 2009, or at any other time.

Sincerely,

Linda S. Jefferson

The Shandler Law Firm, P.C.

February 3, 2009

J. Morgan Dumont, III
P. O. Box 266
Holicong, Pennsylvania 18928-0266

Dear Mr. Dumont:

I have received and read your letter dated January 28, 2009. Most assuredly, I can be of service to you and your mother in planning her estate. I agree with you that the federal estate tax is the most onerous tax imposed on Americans, and I applaud your research attempts in finding a method whereby you and your mother can minimize the tax burden imposed upon her death.

While I admire the ingenuity of your current plan to avoid the federal estate tax, I am not at all convinced that such a drastic step is necessary. There are several ways to form "offshore" trusts and accounts that do provide significant income and estate tax benefits. Your mother could set up such an arrangement, which would not require a marriage. However, I also want to caution you that there are many illegal, and therefore ineffective, ways to set up offshore trusts and accounts.

I am grateful to our mutual acquaintance who referred you to me, but without knowing more, I cannot be sure how much information you have concerning my practice. I currently spend 80 – 85 % of my time doing estate planning. Mr. Dumont, I look forward to working with you and your mother. Please do not hesitate to call me at your earliest convenience with questions or concerns. I am available to meet with you and your mother, either at my offices or a location closer to you and your mother.

Very truly yours,

Great!! Hire this lawyer!!

David R. Shandler, Attorney at Law

███████████, Suite ████ Williamsport, Pennsylvania 17701 • (570)████████ • Fax (570)████████
E-mail: ████████████████.net

MEMBER OF THE AMERICAN ACADEMY OF ESTATE PLANNING ATTORNEYS

J. MORGAN DUMONT, III

POST OFFICE BOX 266
HOLICONG, PENNSYLVANIA 18901

February 19, 2009

David R. Shandler, Esq.
██████████ Suite ████
Williamsport, Pennsylvania 17701

CONFIDENTIAL

Dear Mr. Shandler:

Thank you for your well thought-out reply. Of course, I've considered the utilization of a trust, but Mother wants me to have the money outright so that I can have unfettered use of it. Placing the estate assets in trust imposes too many restrictions on me.

As to what happens upon my death to these assets, I couldn't care less. I have no heirs, and I fully intend to spend every nickel before it's my time to shed this veil of tears. In other words, if 100% of the money goes to Uncle Sam upon my death, so be it. Under these circumstances, I think marrying Mother makes the most sense.

Mother and I have registered as Truk residents, and we have already applied for our marriage license. We are determined to get married in order to make sure that the IRS won't be taking me to the cleaners when Mother dies. However, we still need advice as to whether carnal relations are necessary in order to defeat the government's possible contention that our union should be declared void.

I would like you to meet Mother and me on March 2, 2009, at 4:00 P.M. I'm not from Williamsport, but Mother is. I'll be flying my private plane to your local airport and will be arriving at 3:00 P.M. Mother has an appointment for her final fitting for her wedding gown at bridal shop downtown at 3:30 P.M. In order to make another pressing engagement, I'll have to fly out no later than 5:30 P.M. I'm sorry that our meeting with you has to be so short.

In light of my tight schedule, Mother won't have time to change back into her everyday clothing. Therefore, I ask you to make allowances for the fact that Mother will have to wear her gown when we meet at your office.

Perhaps at the meeting, you can advise us about whether we must consummate our upcoming union. Lately, Mother (who has always been a staunch liberal) has been acting practically Victorian about the subject. The only saving grace is that she likes being a bride again. She says it makes her feel 70 years younger. I have one simple request. When you see Mother, could you make a fuss over her gown and engagement ring? I'm trying hard to maintain her enthusiasm for our marriage.

I look forward to meeting you.

Very truly yours,

J. Morgan Dumont

J. Morgan Dumont

The Shandler Law Firm, P.C.

March 3, 2009

J. Morgan Dumont, III
P. O. Box 266
Holicong, Pennsylvania 18928-0266

Dear Mr. Dumont:

As our appointment was not kept, I hope nothing serious has happened to you or your mother. I remained in my office until my usual departure time, around 5:30 p.m., but left thereafter. I hope you did not come to the office and find me not there.

Please call to reschedule the appointment. I have several issues I would like to discuss with you and your mother concerning the plan for her estate.

I look forward to hearing from you soon.

Sincerely,

David R. Shandler
Attorney at Law

Suite ██ *Williamsport, Pennsylvania 17701* • (570)████ • *Fax* (570)████
E-mail: ████.net

MEMBER OF THE AMERICAN ACADEMY OF ESTATE PLANNING ATTORNEYS

J. MORGAN DUMONT, III

POST OFFICE BOX 266
HOLICONG, PENNSYLVANIA 18901

March 9, 2009

David R. Shandler, Esq.
████████ Suite██
Williamsport, Pennsylvania 17701

CONFIDENTIAL

Dear Mr. Shandler:

I am very sorry that my appointment with you was not kept, but I hope that you will understand why Mother and I couldn't meet with you as planned.

As you know, the day of our appointment, Mother was being fitted with her wedding gown. Everything was going well, and Mother seemed excited about her wedding dress, slips, etc. Just before we were ready to leave the store, the shop keeper insisted on showing Mother lingerie for our wedding night. She came to Mother's dressing room and held up a pair of bright red, sheer panties that were, to say the least, highly provocative. Mother started hyperventilating. She passed out and was raced by ambulance to the hospital.

Apparently, the shock of visualizing herself on our wedding night wearing such intentionally enticing, risqué lingerie caused her to suffer a stroke. She's alert and recovering now and is being pampered in her private hospital suite. Nevertheless, the incident underscored the urgency of resolving the inheritance tax problem immediately.

Because of Mother's frail health and advanced age, I decided that I can't afford to take the risk of waiting for trust instruments, wills and the like to be researched and drafted. Since my plan to marry Mother was in progress at the time of her stroke, I decided to expedite my arrangements. I am therefore having a native holy man from Truk flown on my private jet to the hospital where Mother is recuperating. If all goes well, Mother and I will be married in the hospital chapel next week.

In an odd way, it seems that Mother's stroke was meant to be. As you know, I was concerned that carnal relations with Mother might jeopardize her health. Now that the wedding night will be celebrated in her private hospital room, she'll be just a few feet away from immediate medical care if our love making proves too exhausting.

I sincerely regret that Mother's recent health problems forced me to pursue a plan of action that circumvented you. Be assured that I greatly appreciated your eagerness to assist me with the inheritance tax matter. If you have any tax suggestions that I should consider as Mother's new husband, I would appreciate hearing from you.

Very truly yours,

J. Morgan Dumont

J. Morgan Dumont

JMD/km

NO REPLY!

CHAPTER 2

Mr. Dumont's Magnificent Redwoods

J. MORGAN DUMONT, III

POST OFFICE BOX 192
MECHANICSVILLE, PENNSYLVANIA 18934-0192

June 1, 2009

Gregory T. Gibson, Esq.
Gibson, Greer & Anderson
████████████████████
P.O. Box ██████████
██████████Ohio ██████

CONFIDENTIAL

Dear Mr. Gibson:

A mutual acquaintance has given me your name. I need the help of a lawyer to assist me with an enterprise that promises to be incredibly lucrative. I realize that the services of a good litigator are not cheap, and I am prepared to pay an up front, non-refundable flat fee of $350,000 to the lawyer who I select. (I don't like paying lawyers by the hour because it encourages inefficiency and waste.) Although I realize that sophisticated litigation often costs more than $350,000, I thought that you might nevertheless be tempted to take my case if I paid a flat fee up front.

I need to set forth the background facts if you are to help me. I am the only surviving direct descendant of the famous realist painter, François Dumont. He was remarkably adventurous for his time. In 1829, he sailed to the New World, crossed the Isthmus of Panama and sailed to present day California. There, he painted several famous scenes of the Pacific Northwest that he brought back to Europe. He was particularly captivated by the giant coastal redwoods that dwarfed the largest trees that any European had ever seen. All of his paintings from that trip feature these giant coastal redwoods. His paintings created a sensation in France, and many critics there did not believe that such a magnificent landscape could exist, and they chastised him for abandoning realism and "reverting" to the style of the Romantics.

The sensation that François Dumont created crossed the Atlantic and caught the attention of the Mexican government. Between 1832 and 1835, the Mexican government issued land grants in its province of California to political favorites. In 1833, Valetín Gómez Farías, Mexico's Vice President, who served under the famous

President and General, Santa Anna, heard of the Dumont sequoia landscapes of (then) Mexico's territory. It was a period of the most intense nationalism in Mexico, and the magnificent scenery of that country's most distant province was the subject of national pride. Farías offered to grant a magnificent coastal sequoia grove to François Dumont if he gave one of his sequoia paintings to the Mexican people. François Dumont agreed, and Mexico granted him title to a coastal sequoia grove northwest of present-day San Francisco.

Upon François Dumont's death in 1838, he devised his California property to his eldest son, Jacques Dumont. Late in life, Jacques Dumont became the French Ambassador to the United States during the French Third Republic. While in Washington, D.C., he sold the magnificent sequoia grove, which was then located in the State of California, to William Kent, an American Congressman. However, the deed conveyed the land only. The mineral and timber rights were expressly reserved by that deed and by another contemporaneously drawn instrument that was recorded with the appropriate hall of records in California. Today, the mineral and timber rights belong to me, J. Morgan Dumont, the last surviving descendant of Jacques Dumont.

In 1908, Congressman William Kent and his wife conveyed the sequoia grove to the United States of America. The deed recited that the Kents conveyed to the people of the United States. . .

"all [their] rights, title and interest, in and to the subject Property, that the grantors herein had acquired pursuant to a certain Deed, excluding certain rights reserved by [their] predecessor-in-title as set forth in a certain Deed executed, sealed and delivered unto [us] by The Honorable Jacques Dumont on the 18th day of April, in the year of Our Lord eighteen hundred and eighty-eight."

(Parenthetically, I found it interesting that Congressman and Mrs. Kent were apparently mindful of the fact that they could not convey the property in fee simple absolute). President Theodore Roosevelt created the Muir Woods National Monument out of their donation. Today, it is one of the most visited national monuments because it is one of the last few remaining primeval sequoia groves in the world.

The Muir Woods National Monument is only about 503 acres, but it is crammed with the largest coastal redwoods in the World, many of which exceed 300 feet in height and 15 feet in diameter. Redwood is expensive timber, and just one tree will yield an amazing number of boards. Each mature tree (about 2,000 years old) is worth a fortune. The Muir Woods National Monument contains several hundred of such ancient trees.

I want to be compensated for my timber rights. To that end, I've asked a prominent property lawyer to research the law for me. After analyzing an exhaustive title search, he confirmed that my rights to the timber have not been affected by past conveyances. Moreover, he assured me that the federal government is constitutionally prohibited from taking my timber rights without paying just compensation. However, this property lawyer advised me that a property owner cannot be compelled to purchase mineral or timber rights that attach to his property. Therefore, there is no cause of action against the United States to compel it to pay me.

In order to get compensated, the United States would have to voluntarily agree to contract to buy my timber rights. Even if I could get the feds to talk to me, the bureaucrats in Washington would undoubtedly negotiate for years, wear me down both financially and emotionally, and, in the end, offer a mere pittance instead of equitable compensation. The government's attitude will undoubtedly be that I should be grateful for any compensation at all since it has no legal obligation to buy my timber rights.

In order to get the government's attention, I have decided that it is necessary to act in a way that is consistent with my rights. I'm going to wait for a rainy winter day when there are few if any people visiting the Muir Woods National Monument. At that time, I will bring in a crew of lumberjacks and cut down a dozen or so of the largest trees. I've already hired these men and have promised them handsome compensation for cutting down the best redwood specimens. Obviously, we'll be stopped by National Park Police after several trees are felled, and the federal government will undoubtedly obtain an emergency injunction against me. However, after the dust settles, they'll realize that I'm serious about exercising my timber rights, and the public, as well as "tree huggers" like Al Gore, will demand that the government pay me whatever it takes to protect their precious sequoias. That's the only way to get fair compensation. My course is irrevocably set. All I need now is to retain a lawyer who isn't afraid to fight the federal government.

Because these trees are beloved by Californians, I realize that I need a lawyer outside of that State to represent me once I am enjoined by the government from cutting down more trees. (I suspect that nature-neurotic Californians will thereafter boycott any attorney from their State that takes up my cause). That is why I've written to you. I understand that since the action would be venued in federal court, the fact that you are licensed in a State other than California shouldn't matter since (I am told) the litigation rules among different federal courts are very similar.

I am interviewing one other lawyer, and I am asking both of you to give me your written preliminary thoughts as to what litigation strategy you would employ as well as your brief analysis of the issues. I will review and compare your replies in determining which lawyer should be retained. Kindly correspond with me promptly.

Very truly yours,

J. Morgan Dumont, III

JMD/km

P.S. I would, undoubtedly, stand to make a much bigger profit if I could clear cut the Muir Woods National Monument instead of simply selling my timber rights. Although I've given up this idea as being impractical, I'm open to any creative ideas that you might have to effectuate this goal. Thank you.

Gibson, Greer & Anderson

A Legal Professional Association

Andrew W. Gibson
Laura R. Greer
Charles R. Anderson
Arnold Kross

June 22, 2009

J. Morgan Dumont, III
P. O. Box 192
Mechanicsville, Pennsylvania 18934-0198

Dear Mr. Dumont, III:

Thank you for your request for me to consider representing you in your intriguing property rights claim. I appreciate the confidence you have placed in me, or in our mutual acquaintance's recommendation. The facts in support of your claim, and the manner in which you presented them to me, are most interesting.

The formulation of a specific legal strategy to pursue your claim is dependent on a large number of factors. First, what is the strength of your claim that the mineral and timber rights were not conveyed to Congressman Kent with the conveyance of land?

Second, I would need to examine any U.S. and California statutes and case law that may intrude upon or confuse the rights of private ownership of mineral and timber interests to property otherwise conveyed to government.

Third, I would need to consider what additional arguments or defenses could be offered up by the government, based upon the lack of law or statehood at the time of the original conveyances, or any latches or unnecessary delay arguments that may attach to the failure of your predecessor family members in the chain of title from Jacques Dumont to you to act upon these rights up to now.

Fourth, what is the strength of your own claim of ownership of the rights reserved by Jacques Dumont? By what instruments have such rights been conveyed, transferred, assigned, or inherited by you? What competing claims may intrude upon your position as the "last surviving descendent" and therefore the heir of Jacques Dumont and rightful owner of these rights?

████████████ **P.O. BOX** ████████████ **Ohio** ████████
Phone (740) ████████ **Fax (740)** ████████

Gibson, Greer & Anderson
A Legal Professional Association

Finally, I would need to examine what venue (which court where) may be most conducive to the success of your efforts and what means of advocacy creates the best outcome for you.

The cut a few first/litigate afterwards strategy decision you have made in response to your property lawyer's advice may injure, rather than advance, your cause. It will undoubtedly secure the government's attention for your claim and notoriety for you. This may be good or bad, depending on its alignment with your overall case strategy. However, it may make your first round of litigation the defense of criminal charges against you or your crew, or litigation against you by your crew after their own criminal prosecution, as what you propose to do may be a criminal act under state or federal law. Even if your property rights defense is successful, it may be high stakes, high risk, and not how you want to spend your first year of effort on this claim. It may also dig the heels of government in against you in what otherwise may have been a claim that could have been settled, rather than litigated and appealed for years.

If your "course is irrevocably set" for a particular case strategy before engaging and conferring with the legal counsel who will represent you to together identify your best course of action, then I am not the attorney to work with you. My process requires an agreed upon and understood case strategy and working partnership to achieve a specific goal. If your "course is irrevocably set" more generally to fight the federal government to be fairly compensated for the rights that have been reserved for you by your family predecessors, and you seek to engage counsel to help you identify and put into action the best means to achieve that goal, then I will be glad to explore with you further whether we should join resources for this purpose.

I have enjoyed considering your inquiry and look forward to hearing from you on how you would like to proceed.

Best regards,

Andrew W. Gibson

Great!!
Hire this lawyer!!

P.O. BOX Ohio
Phone (740) **Fax (740)**

J. MORGAN DUMONT, III

POST OFFICE BOX 192
MECHANICSVILLE, PENNSYLVANIA 18934-0192

June 26, 2009

Gregory W. Gibson, Esq.
Gibson, Greer & Anderson
████████████████████████████

P.O. Box ███████
████████ Ohio ████████

CONFIDENTIAL

Dear Mr. Gibson:

I am in receipt of your exhaustive letter of June 20, 2009. Well done. I agree with almost all of your conclusions, but I want to address one assumption in your letter that is, candidly, just plain wrong.

In your letter, you state that my "cut a few first/litigate afterwards strategy" will "undoubtedly secure the government's attention for [my] claim and notoriety for [me]." With this conclusion, I whole-heartedly agree. However, my disagreement lies in your next sentence, in which you state that my "cut first" strategy "may be good or bad, depending upon its alignment with [my] overall case strategy." You then entreat me not to cut first and sue later because this strategy might subject me to criminal prosecution.

You incorrectly imply that I am so spineless as to be intimidated by threats of incarceration. I've already spent many years in the can in both federal and state systems. I'm not afraid of facing a little jail time. Besides, except for one experience that I had in a 23-hour lock-up facility, prison life is, in many ways, easier than life on the outside.

Having cleared the air as to this issue, let me state that I am still willing to be flexible and I will remain open-minded as to our prospective strategy.

The flaw that I perceive in your pedestrian strategy of simply applying for a logging permit is that it will not galvanize the American people against the government. A buzzing chain saw, not a denied logging permit, will activate the nature nuts who believe that these trees are priceless. Tree huggers will demand that the government compensate me fairly in order to protect their precious plants by keeping the issue of my timber rights out of the hands of some do-as-you-please judge who might side with me and permit the clear cutting of the Muir Woods. (Although I am a layman, I consider myself an expert on the subject of judicial caprice, since I have been the subject of more than one sentence that exceeded the recommendations of my prosecutors.)

In mid-July, I will be visiting a friend in Marion, Ohio. Sometime during my visit, I'll travel to Athens and drop in to consult with you. I look forward to meeting you and trust that we will be able to enter into a mutually lucrative relationship.

Very truly yours,

J. Morgan Dumont

J. Morgan Dumont, III

Gibson, Greer & Anderson

A Legal Professional Association

Andrew W. Gibson
Laura R. Greer
Charles R. Anderson
Arnold Kross

July 6, 2009

J. Morgan Dumont, III
P.O. Box 192
Mechanicsville, Pennsylvania 18934-0198

Dear J. Morgan Dumont, III

Thank you for your June 26, 2009 letter. I will be away from my office for most of July 7-21, 2009. If that is the period of time you will be visiting your friend in Marion, let my office know and we can set up a time and place to meet in northern Ohio, rather than here. I will be 60-70 miles from Marion at Lake Erie.

It will be interesting to discover if the government has any idea of the serious gap in its rights of ownership, if unknown then why something so important is unknown, or if known, is it intentionally being kept quiet with the hope that you don't act upon your rights. I remain intrigued with your proposed claim and the style with which you present it in your written correspondence with me. At the same time, it is unusual to be in dialogue to date only in writing. A meeting is the right next step in deciding if and how we may choose to work together in this matter.

Sincerely,

Andrew W. Gibson

P.O. BOX ██████ Ohio ██████
Phone (740) ██████ Fax (740) ██████

J. MORGAN DUMONT, III

POST OFFICE BOX 192
MECHANICSVILLE, PENNSYLVANIA 18934-0192

July 23, 2009

Andrew W. Gibson, Esq.
Gibson, Greer & Anderson

P.O. Box

Ohio

CONFIDENTIAL

Dear Mr. Gibson:

Thank you for your letter of July 6. Please let me explain why I have communicated with you in writing only. For all practical purposes, I am deaf. Unless you have a phone that is linked to a computer and video monitor that so that I can read your lips, I can't communicate over telephone lines. However, it's been said that I am such a good lip reader that Mr. Mumbles himself can't slip a word past me, so you needn't be concerned about discussing this matter in person when we meet.

I am grateful for your insights contained in your last correspondence. It jolted me into facing the ugly reality that the federal government has intentionally concealed from me its "serious gap in its rights of ownership". Your letter made me realize that they've played me for a fool. Now I'm livid, and I am determined to make Uncle Sam suffer for his bad faith.

If I own the timber rights, I assume that I can do anything I want to the trees provided that I don't disturb the government's right to use the land. This conclusion, together with a recent visit to Disney World's "Tree of Life" exhibit, gave me inspiration for a special way to profit from my timber rights at the Muir Woods National Monument.

Thousands of adults have held onto their childhood dream of living like Tarzan high up in a fancy tree house, and there are even companies that specialize in constructing tree houses that are used as weekend retreats. It might not be for you or me, but the concept of living in the forest canopy appeals to nature nuts as well as to those with weird, romantic notions of primitive, simple living. Why not turn the forest into a resort community of fancy tree houses? Perhaps I can turn them into timeshare condominiums and really make a killing. After all, once you've cut the tree down, all its value is immediately used up, but turning the sequoias into vacation timeshares could create enormous cash cows that can be milked for decades. Best of all, making each sequoia into a rentable condo will undoubtedly enrage our lying, deceitful government even more than if I clear cut their precious park.

I have enclosed my own artistic conception of one such redwood tree house/timeshare. My only problem is figuring out whether the service elevator for each tree can be built directly on the roots (which I own), since the government can keep me from placing the elevators on its land. I will be consulting an engineer to get a resolution of this technical issue.

What do you think about my unique way of exercising my timber rights? Do you see any legal obstacles of proceeding with the timeshare venture? Please advise. Also, kindly provide me with dates and times when we can meet. I will be happy to travel to your office at your convenience. Thank you. I look forward to meeting you.

Very truly yours,

J. Morgan Dumont

J. Morgan Dumont, III

JMD/km

NO REPLY!

CLARKE & SHANLEY, PLLC
A T T O R N E Y S   A T   L A W

RAND CLARKE
GENE SHANLEY
CYNTHIA FARRIS
J. BRUCE NOVOTNY
CARRIE BURNS
BRIAN W. CONNLLEY
GENE T. JACK
GABRIELLE MCMICHAEL

June 12, 2009

J. Morgan Dumont, III
P. O. Box 192
Mechanicsville, Pennsylvania 18934-0198

Dear Mr. Dumont:

I am receipt of your June 1 letter regarding your claim to Muir Woods. Before I moved to Washington, I grew up in and around those woods and could not in good conscience assist you in any plan to cut down even a few of those trees. I do not practice real estate law, so I am unable to advise you as to the chain of title or adverse possession issues involved in your case.

I do assist people whose trees have been illegally cut down by others. Perhaps that is how you got my name. I cannot advise you as to if, when, or how you might be able to pursue any type of legal claim.

Sincerely,

Brian W. Connelly

BWC:kkn

J. MORGAN DUMONT, III

POST OFFICE BOX 192
MECHANICSVILLE, PENNSYLVANIA 18934-0192

June 22, 2009

Brian W. Connelly, Esq.
Clarke & Shanley, PLLC
████████████████
████████████
Bellingham, WA 98227

CONFIDENTIAL

Dear Mr. Connelly:

I am in receipt of your letter of June 12, 2009. Thank you. In your letter, you state that you could not in good conscience assist me in cutting down even "a few" of the giant redwoods in the Muir Woods. I get the point. Cutting down just one tree, provided that it's one of the largest, will probably suffice and won't get people unduly upset. Good thinking.

It was by no means an accident that I sought you out. To be candid, I hired you because of your reputation as a "tree hugger." Please don't be offended, but I thought that it would give my cause more credibility if a nature neurotic were representing me instead of some flashy lawyer who represents big lumber.

I would like to meet with you in order to see if we can amplify on your idea of cutting down a single large specimen. I will be in Seattle during the first week of July on another matter. I'll use that opportunity to travel to your office. If all goes well, I'll tender to you the non-refundable retainer.

Very truly yours,

J. Morgan Dumont

J. Morgan Dumont, III

JMD/km

CLARKE & SHANLEY, PLLC
ATTORNEYS AT LAW

RAND CLARKE
GENE SHANLEY
CYNTHIA FARRIS
J. BRUCE NOVOTNY
CARRIE BURNS
BRIAN W. CONNLLEY
GENE T. JACK
GABRIELLE MCMICHAEL

June 26, 2009

J. Morgan Dumont, III
P. O. Box 192
Mechanicsville, Pennsylvania 18934-0192

Dear Mr. Dumont:

I am greatly concerned by your letter to me of June 22, 2009. You have completely misinterpreted my previous correspondence to you. I absolutely do NOT recommend that you cut down a single tree. Under no circumstances should you give anyone the impression that I have ever recommended that you destroy federal property. If you have represented to anyone that I have advised you to start logging in a national park, you must immediately disabuse that person of that impression.

Sincerely,

Brian W. Connelly

BWC:kkn

J. MORGAN DUMONT, III

POST OFFICE BOX 192
MECHANICSVILLE, PENNSYLVANIA 18934-0192

July 6, 2009

VIA FEDERAL EXPRESS
Brian W. Connelly, Esq.
Clarke & Shanley, PLLC
████████████████
████████████
Bellingham, WA 98227

CONFIDENTIAL

Dear Mr. Connelly:

Your letter of June 27th stunned me. I spent the July 4th holiday racking my brain to understand why you flip flopped on your brilliant strategy of cutting down one of the largest sequoia specimens at the Muir Woods National Monument. Now I get it. The Feds must be reading your mail, too. Your last letter was a clever red herring that will throw the FBI off the scent and thereby preserve the element of surprise when it comes time for us to bring chainsaws into the park. Good thinking.

As you can see from this letter, I've decided to deliver mail to you via a private courier so that the FBI can't easily get their hands on our private communications. I suggest you do the same. By the way, I won't breathe a word about your logging advice concerning the Muir Woods. Don't worry. When it comes to litigation, I'm pretty sophisticated, and I wouldn't jeopardize the privilege that attaches to our attorney-client communications by divulging your "chop now, negotiate later" advice.

I'll be dropping into your office within the next three weeks. I suggest that I arrive around noon, and we'll have lunch together at a restaurant. In case the FBI has your office under surveillance, (which they probably do), the Feds won't have enough time to plant in their snooping equipment if we choose a restaurant at the spur of the moment. In that way, you'll be able to expound safely on your proposed single-specimen logging strategy at the Muir Woods. I look forward to meeting you.

Very truly yours,

J. Morgan Dumont

J. Morgan Dumont

NO REPLY!

United States Department of the Interior
NATIONAL PARK SERVICE
Pacific West Region
Pacific Land Resources Program Center
600 Harrison Street, Suite 600
San Francisco, California 94107-1372

IN REPLY REFER TO:

L1425 (PWR-OL)
MUWO General
JUL 5
J. Morgan Dumont, III
P.O. Box 192
Mechanicsville, Pennsylvania 18934-0192

Dear Mr. Dumont:

We have received information to the effect that you feel that you own timber rights within Muir Woods National Monument, California. You evidently base this on the effect of a 1888 deed from a Mr. Jacques Dumont to Mr. William Kent, which, while conveying the land which is now at least part of Muir Woods National Monument, reserved to the Grantor the rights to the timber.

This office is willing to look into the question of your possible interest in any timber rights within Muir Woods. If you wish our assistance, please supply us with copies of: 1) The Deed upon which you might base such an assertion; and 2) Evidence sufficient to establish that you are the sole descendant of Mr. Jacques Dumont, and therefore that you are the party with whom we should be dealing.

Muir Woods National Monument is indeed a special unit of the National Park System, and its many resources, in particular its outstanding Coast Redwoods, are worthy of the most stringent protection. It would certainly be a very serious criminal matter for anyone to take unilateral action which might negatively impact such park resources, and it would be action against which the National Park Service would respond forcefully.

If you wish further information or have any questions, please contact Nicholas Whelan of my staff at (415) 427-1413; after July 16, 2001, the telephone number will be changed to (510) 817-1413. Thank you in advance for your cooperation.

Sincerely,

Sondra S. Humphries
Chief, Pacific West Land Resources Program Center

CC: Superintendent, Golden Gate National Recreation Area
Supervisory Park Ranger, Muir Woods National Monument

WILSON FARNSWORTH MANG & JONES, P.C.
ATTORNEYS AT LAW

, Suite
Denver, Colorado 80202
Telephone: 303-
Facsimile: 303-
E-mail: com

Robert P. Wilson
Daniel P. Farnsworth
Rebecca E. Mang
Norman D. Jones
Molly Corbin-Jones
William R. Early
Francis G. O'Brien

Special Counsel
John F. McKee

June 8, 2009

J. Morgan Dumont, III
P. O. Box 192
Mechanicsville, Pennsylvania 18934-0192

Dear Mr. Dumont:

I received your June 1, 2009 letter. First, let me say that it is not possible that we could have a mutual acquaintance. Second, I certainly agree that you need counseling. Your fears that the Federal government would wear you down financially and emotionally are certainly well-founded. Rather than paying for legal representation, I suggest that you simply turn yourself in to the Federal government. Finally, I regret to inform you that I have a conflict of interest which will prohibit me from taking your case. You see, I take the long view of Darwin's theory and I am convinced the redwoods are my direct relatives.

Yours truly,

FRANCIS G. O'BRIEN

P.S. This letter is printed on recycled paper.

CHAPTER 3

Mr. Dumont's Eviction Action

J. MORGAN DUMONT, III

6901 W. OKEECHOBEE BLVD., D-5, BOX 161
WEST PALM BEACH, FLORIDA 33411

January 6, 2009

Phillip W. Sands, Esq.
███████████████████

Daytona Beach, FL 32118

CONFIDENTIAL

Dear Mr. Sands:

A mutual acquaintance recommended that I contact you. I want to commence a lawsuit, and I need to retain a trial lawyer. I realize that serious litigation is not cheap, and I am prepared to pay a non-refundable flat fee of $200,000 to the lawyer who I select. (I don't like paying professionals by the hour because it encourages inefficiency and waste.) Although I realize that sophisticated litigation often costs more than $200,000, I thought that you might nevertheless be tempted to take my case if I paid a flat fee up front.

I cannot over-emphasize the seriousness of this matter. In order for you to assist me, you will need to know all the relevant facts. I am the great-grandson of a famous financier, and my family ranks as one of the wealthiest in America. As a result, I had the good fortune to be raised insulated from vulgar society. I realize that it is fashionable to advocate egalitarianism, but I make no excuses for saying that I am grateful to have been born a Patrician. As a result of my family's high station, I grew up appreciating fine arts and gracious living. I can't imagine living any other way.

I hope the following doesn't offend you, and I trust that, as a lawyer, you are prepared to represent clients whose personal views might conflict with your own. I, like Thomas Jefferson, believe that the colored races are inferior to Caucasians. Don't misunderstand me. For practical reasons, I am not advocating the return of slavery, but I do believe that the races should be kept separate. I tell you this as a necessary prelude to my dilemma.

Recently, I was diagnosed with cancer of the liver, and the best oncologists in the country agree that my condition is terminal. I will survive for only three or four months at most. I have lived a long life and I am emotionally prepared to depart this earth. Because my family crypt is full, it became necessary for me to find an alternative place for my eternal rest.

After a search lasting several weeks, the Grand Master of the gentlemen's club of which I am a founding member recommended an above-ground internment facility that was perfectly suited for someone of my social attainment. The facility is not advertised and does not even have a telephone number. It is nestled in a secluded country estate. The facility, called The Necrotheon of Olympus (the "Necrotheon"), caters to the affluent and offers luxurious vaults and perpetual care. The mausoleum itself is styled as a Greek temple which is sculpted from the finest Italian marble. It will serve as a memorial befitting of my rank. Because I am a bachelor and do not have children or surviving family members, it was only necessary that I reserve a single vault for myself. When I learned that the Necrotheon was in such demand among my peers that it had just one vault remaining, I immediately took action to reserve it.

I interviewed the general manager of the Necrotheon, Mr. Everett Eakins, in order to make sure that my companions-in-death were socially prominent. (This seemed to me to be a safe assumption in light of the substantial purchase price for a single vault). I made it very clear to Mr. Eakins that I did not want to be laid to rest next to any Jews, Arabs, Turks, Mongols or Negroes.

In response, Mr. Eakins represented to me that the deceased in the vaults surrounding mine were only the best people from elite society, and he assured me that none was a Jew, Arab, Turk or Mongol. Mr. Eakins specifically represented that the man who had already been buried to the right of my vault had been a prominent doctor. I checked this representation by looking at the gold memorial plaque on the vault, and sure enough, the man next door had been a doctor by the name of "Elias Washington, M.D." As a result of these representations, I paid the full purchase price for the vault (i.e., $500,000).

Last Sunday, a friend from my club accompanied me to the Necrotheon to see where I would be laid to rest. At that time, we were stunned to see a Colored family visiting the tomb of Elias Washington, M.D. Of course, I demanded to know why they were loitering there, and, to my astonishment, an elderly Negress informed me that they were all family members of the deceased, Dr. Elias Washington.

Naturally, I was enraged by Mr. Eakins' deception. Can you imagine my embarrassment when my friend saw that I would be laid to rest next to a Colored? Obviously, this business about Washington having been a "prominent" physician was a lie. Eakins never mentioned what kind of physician that Washington had been, but my inquiry obviously did not embrace "prominent" African witch doctors.

I can't stand the thought of being laid to rest next to a Negro. The horror of this prospect was brought home when I saw the Washington family in front of Elias Washington's vault. Everyone knows that their kind likes to picnic in cemeteries. This is particularly abhorrent to me since I simply can't stand the sight or smell of fried chicken, and I refuse to be subjected to generation after generation of Washingtons munching on deep fried bird carcasses in front of me.

Mr. Eakins refuses to give me my money back. He says that as a real estate salesman, it would have been illegal to "steer" me to a different vault. Perhaps this is so, but Eakins did more than decline to steer me. In order to make the sale, Eakins deceived me into believing that I would not be laid to rest next to a racially undesirable. Isn't this fraud? I mean, I made it very clear to Eakins that I would not purchase a vault if I would be interred next to a Negro.

I am looking for a lawyer to sue for either my money back or for a judicial order requiring the Necrotheon to move Washington's remains away from the vicinity of my vault. (Moving Washington out is my first choice). I only have a few months left to live, and I am desperate.

I am interviewing one other lawyer, and I am asking both of you to give me your written preliminary thoughts as to what litigation strategy you would employ as well as your brief analysis of the issues. I will review and compare your replies in determining which lawyer should be retained. Kindly correspond with me promptly.

Very truly yours,

J. Morgan Dumont

J. Morgan Dumont, III

JMD/km

PHILLIP W. SANDS, P.A.
ATTORNEY AT LAW

▆▆▆▆▆▆▆▆▆▆ AVENUE

DAYTONA BEACH, FLORIDA 32118

BOARD CERTIFIED
CIVIL TRAIL LAWYER

January 12, 2009

J. Morgan Dumont, III
6901 W. Okeechobee Blvd., D-5
West Palm Beach, Fl 33411

Re: Dumont v. Necrotheon of Olympus

Dear Mr. Dumont:

I am in receipt of your letter of 1/6 and in reply have sent you my resume for your review. I would be happy to sue the facility for fraud based upon what you have reported to me. However, before I agree on the price I need to know where the defendant's facility lies (county) for jurisdictional purposes, and some other details. Trial practice is my specialty, and this case sounds very interesting. I believe you have a good case for fraud in the inducement of the contract, and an equally good case for correcting this injustice. I look forward to hearing from you in the near future.

Very truly yours,

Phillip W. Sands

PWS/vc
Encl.

Great!!
Hire this lawyer!!

J. MORGAN DUMONT, III

**6901 W. OKEECHOBEE BLVD., D-5, BOX 161
WEST PALM BEACH, FLORIDA 33411**

January 21, 2009

Phillip W. Sands, Esq.
██████████████████████
Daytona Beach, FL 32118

CONFIDENTIAL

Dear Mr. Sands:

Pain from my cancer is now excruciating, which has in turn intensified my anguish over the prospects of lying in repose throughout eternity next to that loitering Negro in the neighboring crypt. However, when I read that you "would be happy to sue the [Necrotheon] for fraud", and that I "have a good case for fraud in the inducement of the contract, and an equally good case for correcting this injustice", I became practically jubilant. In fact, I momentarily forgot about my pain. I was also pleased to read that you find my problem to be "very interesting" since people always do a better job when they are intellectually engaged by their work. Your resume that you sent to me was the icing on the cake. I'm convinced that you have just the right qualifications necessary to make sure that that African witch doctor, the so-called, "Elias Washington, M.D.", is evicted from the Necrotheon.

Unfortunately, my liver cancer is more aggressive than my oncologist had initially thought, and it has metastasized throughout my body. I am dictating this letter to my secretary from my hospital bed, and I do not expect to be returning home. I've been told that I have only a matter of days left to live, which makes it necessary for us to cement our relationship quickly. Would you be willing to come to the hospital so that I can get my affairs in order? Please let me know as soon as possible.

I have one other request to make, which is admittedly unusual. However, I am prepared to compensate you handsomely for undertaking it. In order to appreciate my request, you will need some factual background.

I am a film buff, and I have always been deeply moved by the classic film, Citizen Kane. Recall that the film begins with the millionaire, Charles Foster Kane, as an old man uttering his dying words, "Rose Bud." The remainder of the film is structured around a newspaper reporter's efforts to discover the meaning of these cryptic words. In the film's final frames, it is revealed that "Rose Bud" was the name of Kane's sled when he was a happy, innocent child not yet hardened and demoralized by life's vicissitudes. Now that my own dissolution is near, Kane's dying words, "Rose Bud", are preoccupying me.

My own particular "Rose Bud" was not a sled but a roller coaster. My parents forbade me from ever visiting any amusement park because they believed that they are the cesspools of the hoi polloi. They didn't want me to demean myself or impugn the honor of my Patrician family by putting a single toe inside one. However, in 1939, my Aunt Suzanne secretly took me to the New York World's Fair. There, I experienced the most exhilarating time of my life when, like Charles Foster Kane, I was shot through with the unadulterated joy of life. I remember the Great Sphere next to the Art Deco towering pyramid, the World of the Future, and the exotic sights and sounds of the International Exhibits. For me, however, the Fair's highlight was its giant, though simple, wooden roller coaster.

For the last 60 years, I've pined for the feel of the vibrating, rickety wooden supports as the coaster is slowly pulled by chains, lurching towards the rails' apex. I remember with longing the thrill of momentarily hanging at the top of the ride for the briefest of seconds just before taking a wild plunge. I've yearned to feel the wind in my hair and hear the squeals of excited children as the coaster car falls from its precipice seemingly out of control. I ache to feel the warmth of my fellow riders as they press against me as the coaster whips around the final tight curve. In short, I have spent the last six decades hungering to relive that sweet day of my youth.

My obsession with recapturing this one day in my life caused me to leave my triplex overlooking New York's Central Park and retire close to Disney World. Even though I've never actually visited the park, just being near Orlando gives me, in some inexplicable way, occasional glimpses of that care-free day when I was more than just happy. I was euphoric. I want to have one last thrilling, rapturous ride.

This is prelude to my special (and admittedly) unusual request. After my passing, I want to take one last ride on Disney Land's "Space Mountain" roller coaster. I have chosen "Space Mountain" because I've been told that it simulates a ride to the heavens—the same trip that I will soon be taking after I take my last breath. My Last Will and Testament instructs my executor to pay the Disney Company up to

$1,000,000.00 for a single ride on its "Space Mountain" roller coaster, on the condition that it is scheduled during normal hours of normal operation. (Half the fun is hearing the laughs and screams of children and feeling the warm press of your coaster companion through the ride's twists and turns).

My nephew, who I have appointed as the executor of my estate, is a good man but a bad negotiator, and I don't trust him to land a deal with the Disney people. Instead, I will amend my will in order to authorize you for the limited purpose of binding my estate to the aforementioned contract. If you agree, I will pay you $100,000.00 for negotiating the contract, and I will give you an additional $100,000.00 if you are successful. The bonus will be conditioned, however, on your agreeing to oversee Disney's performance in order to ensure that my final request is properly honored.

Please let me know immediately if you are willing to perform this additional service for me, since time is running out. Thank you.

Very truly yours,

J. Morgan Dumont, III

JMD/km

PHILLIP W. SANDS, P.A.
ATTORNEY AT LAW
██████████ AVENUE
DAYTONA BEACH, FLORIDA 32118

**BOARD CERTIFIED
CIVIL TRAIL LAWYER**

January 31, 2009

J. Morgan Dumont, III
6901 W. Okeechobee Blvd., D-5
West Palm Beach, Fl 33411

Re: Dumont v. Necrotheon of Olympus

Dear Mr. Dumont:

I am in receipt of your letter of the 21st. Thank you. I will be happy to represent you with respect to negotiating your proposed contract that you have described with the Disney Company. Although there is no guarantee that I will be able to achieve your objective, I will do my very best. Before I undertake this project for you, however, I will need to examine your will in order to make sure that it empowers me with the requisite authority to bind your estate to such a contract.

I need to meet with you immediately in order to consult with you about the action against the Necrotheon and effectuating your final wish. Of course, I will be pleased to visit you where you are hospitalized. To that end, I ask that you or your representative telephone me as soon as you receive this letter so that we can meet.

At the time of our meeting, I will also ask you to sign a retainer agreement. Because you are hospitalized, it will be prudent for me to have that retainer notarized in the presence of a witness who can attest to your competency, since I would not want anyone interested in your estate to successfully argue that your disease had in any way affected your judgment. I look forward to meeting you.

Very truly yours,

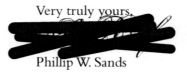

Phillip W. Sands

PWS/vc

MONTESQUIEU M. DUMONT
EXECUTOR OF THE ESTATE OF J. MORGAN DUMONT, III

9663 SANTA MONICA BLVD.,
BOX 274
BEVERLY HILLS, CALIFORNIA 90210-4303

February 2, 2009

Phillip W. Sands, Esq.
███████████
Daytona Beach, FL 32118

Dear Mr. Sands:

I am the Executor of the Estate of my uncle, J. Morgan Dumont, III. It is my sad duty to inform you that Mr. Dumont expired on January 31, 2009. As you know, he was a remarkable man. We who knew and loved him feel the crush of grief. Uncle Morgan understood how many people would be devastated by his passing since so many have relied upon him for his selfless compassion.

True to his nature, my Uncle provided in his Last Will and Testament that the bereaved should receive intensive grief counseling, the cost of which is to be paid by his Estate. Immediately before his passing, Uncle Morgan hastily wrote a codicil to his Last Will and Testament, providing that you should receive such counseling from his own trusted psychiatrist as a special bequest to you. He was the only psychiatrist who was able to get Uncle Morgan's schizophrenia into remission (albeit intermittently), and he is completely trusted by our entire family to help you cope with your own bereavement. (I understand that the same drug therapy he uses in grief counseling also worked wonders in controlling Uncle Morgan's hallucinations.) You should expect to receive a call from Uncle Morgan's psychiatrist shortly. In his Will, my Uncle also made sure that you should not have to be burdened with traveling in order to receive his final gift. Accordingly, his psychiatrist will be making arrangements to provide you with bereavement counseling at your Daytona Beach office.

I regret that I never had the pleasure of knowing you, but I imagine that you and Uncle Morgan were particularly close. In fact, while he was dying and drifting in and out of consciousness, he repeatedly said words to the effect he wanted you to "hold his hand when we ride." I'm unclear as to what that meant. If his words have any resonance with you, please let me know what they mean. In any event, I was comforted to know that he had you, his friend, on his mind at the moment of his passing.

I must delay my Uncle's internment because he instructed me in his Will to orchestrate a rather elaborate funeral and arrange for a special embalming procedure. Accordingly, Uncle Morgan's memorial service will be held on February 23, 2009, at 11:00 a.m. The service will take place at a private mausoleum in Florida known as the Necrotheon of Olympus. (When I receive directions, I will fax them to you).

This brings me to the most important part of this letter. Since you were the one who was in my Uncle's thoughts at the moment of his passing, I think it appropriate that you should pronounce the eulogy, or at the very least, say a few words about how much Uncle Morgan meant to you. Trusting that you will be a true friend to Uncle Morgan even in death, I thank you in advance for participating in the ceremony commemorating a great life.

With warmest regards, I am

Very truly yours,

Montesquieu M. Dumont

Montesquieu M. Dumont

PHILLIP W. SANDS, P.A.

ATTORNEY AT LAW

██████████ AVENUE

Daytona Beach, Florida 32118

BOARD CERTIFIED
CIVIL TRIAL LAWYER

February 9, 2009

Mr. Montesquieu M. Dumont
9663 Santa Monica Blvd.
Box 274
Beverly Hills, CA 90210-4303

Dear Mr. Dumont:

I was saddened to hear the news of your uncle's passing. I know that he suffered before his death, but I suppose that we can take some comfort in knowing that the end came faster than his physicians had originally anticipated.

I was deeply touched that Mr. Dumont was thinking about me when he was taken from us. I am sure you remember your uncle as a very special person. You have my deepest condolences.

I must decline your invitation to eulogize your uncle with my sincerest regrets. I will be conducting a lengthy trial during the weeks surrounding February 23rd when Mr. Dumont will be laid to rest. Unfortunately, it is an obligation that the court will not permit me to postpone. I am greatly honored, however, that you have asked me to speak at his memorial service. Thank you.

Again, you have my sincere condolences for your loss.

Very truly yours,

Phillip W. Sands

PWS/vc

𝕾𝖆𝖓𝖋𝖔𝖗𝖉 𝕽. 𝕾𝖈𝖍𝖜𝖆𝖗𝖙𝖟, 𝕻.𝕬.

ATTORNEY AT LAW

SANDFORD R. SCHWARTZ
(561) ████
(561) ████ **FAX**

CORPORATE CENTRE
SUITE ████
████ **ROAD**
BOCA RATON, FL 33434

January 26, 2009

Mr. J. Morgan Dumont, III
6901 W. Okeechobee Blvd., D-5
Box 161
West Palm Beach, FL 33411

Dear Mr. Dumont:

I was quite intrigued by your correspondence of January 6, 2009. You have asked me to provide my litigation strategy and brief analysis of the issues which I would apply should I be asked to represent you in the matter you described to me. My suggestion would be that you claim insanity and then ask the court to consider your contract null and void since the law does not recognize the capacity of the insane to enter into legal contracts. If successful, you would be entitled to your money back. After reading your correspondence, I believe the court could easily accept an insanity defense to the enforceability of the contract.

Regarding the legal fees which I would charge should I be asked to represent you in this matter, I would handle the case on a pro bono basis and donate all legal fees to the American Jewish Congress with the stipulation that any recovery would be donated to the National Association for the Advancement of Colored People in order to combat the type of racism which is evident in your letter

Sincerely,

Sanford R. Schwartz

J. MORGAN DUMONT, III

6901 W. OKEECHOBEE BLVD., D-5, BOX 161
WEST PALM BEACH, FLORIDA 33411

February 11, 2009

Sanford R. Schwartz, Esq.

███████████

███████████

Boca Raton, FL 33434██████

CONFIDENTIAL

Dear Mr. Schwartz:

Thank you for your reply letter of January 25, 2009. I was astonished that you are familiar with the pathology of liver cancer and that you know that it can metastasize and invade the central nervous system, thereby causing dementia. Although my cancer has not yet reached that stage, it's a very clever ploy to use against the owners and operators of the Necrotheon in order to get around the contract. I congratulate you.

I have one question, however. How will the insanity ploy help me get a vault located away from Elias Washington? I might be wrong, but don't we have to do more than avoid the contract? I want to be laid to rest at the Necrotheon, but not next to an undesirable.

I thought your gimmick about telling the world that you would be donating the proceeds to the NAACP was a stroke of genius. It's sad that our society has devolved to the state in which we have to worry about appeasing left-wing judges, but I am at least gratified that you're looking out for my interests.

I was, candidly, taken aback by the irritated tone that you took in the conclusion of your letter. After I read it, I reviewed my first correspondence in order to ascertain what caused you to react in such a negative way. Then I re-read the sentence in my letter about not wanting to be buried next to an Arab, Turk or Jew. I'm sorry. I meant to take out that reference in the version of the letter that I sent to you, but my proofreading was somewhat sloppy.

At least I hope you will accept this explanation: Although I would not want to be buried next to a Jew, I would never hesitate to have one as my legal advocate. Your clever strategies laid out in your responsive letter amply prove that you people are naturals when it comes to the law and vindicates my decision to ask for your guidance.

Unless it is inconvenient for you, I'll be visiting your office for an interview on February 24, 2009, at 2:00 P.M. I look forward to meeting you.

Very truly yours,

J. Morgan Dumont

Sanford R. Schwartz, P.A.
ATTORNEY AT LAW

BARRY SILVER
(561) ███████
(561) ██████FAX

CORPORATE CENTRE
SUITE █████
███████ ROAD
BOCA RATON, FL 33434

February 16, 2009

Mr. J. Morgan Dumont, III
6901 W. Okeechobee Blvd., D-5
Box 161
West Palm Beach, FL 33411

Dear Mr. Dumont:

I have your last letter, and on reconsideration, perhaps I was too harsh in my judgment of you. I now sympathize with your suffering, and lament the fact that you have only three or four months left in which to live. Unfortunately, I am solidly booked for many months, and I can't squeeze you in for an interview on February 24 as you have requested. My first available appointment is on Monday, September 25, 2009, at 9:00 a.m. I think that date will be convenient for both of us, so I've marked it on my calendar. See you then!

Sincerely,

Sanford R. Schwartz

CHAPTER 4

Mr. Dumont and the Dalai Lama

CONFIDENTIAL

J. MORGAN DUMONT, III

9663 SANTA MONICA BLVD., BOX 274
BEVERLY HILLS, CALIFORNIA 90210-4303

December 6, 2007

Andrew Simpson, Esq.
Rosenblatt & Simpson, P.C.
▬▬▬▬▬▬▬▬▬▬▬▬▬
▬▬▬▬▬▬
Los Angeles, California 90067

CONFIDENTIAL

Dear Mr. Simpson:

I'm in terrible trouble, and a mutual acquaintance has urged me to contact you. The background to my problem is a bit complicated and difficult to convey orally in an organized fashion. Therefore, I thought that it would be prudent to put the facts down on paper first so that you can more easily analyze my problem.

When I was stationed in India while in the service of the Royal Marines during World War II, I became enraptured by Eastern religions. I was fascinated by the contemplative disciplines taught in both Hindu and Buddhist traditions. The elaborate mythology of Sikhism and the non-violent tradition of Jainism has left an indelible mark on me.

After my discharge from His Majesty's Royal Marines, I emigrated to the United States at which time I promptly enrolled in the American Society of Transcendentalism and Eastern Mysticism. We meet in a clubhouse for a former golf course that has since been developed for residential housing.

For fifty years, I have been the most uneducated member of our Society, and the holders of doctorate degrees, university professors and enlightened clergymen have always looked down on me. For example, not once since I joined the Society have I ever been allowed to lay the garland wreath at our shrine of Vishnu. Because I have a lisp, my fellow members forbid me to recite the Sacred Mantra Summoning Sinless Souls — the prerequisite set by our Society's spiritual leader to the attainment of Cosmic Unification. The final humiliation came during our society's celebration of the birth of Siddhartha, and for an entire month, we imposed the cast system on our membership. Needless to state, I was designated as our Society's only untouchable.

I realize that one of the goals of Eastern religions is the subordination of the ego, but I have to be honest with you. I grew damn tired of standing on the bottom rung. For the last five years, I've thought of doing something special at the Society that would give me recognition and respect. Finally, last month, while listening to the car radio, I found it.

The announcer said that for a flat engagement fee of $20,000, the Dalai Lama would appear for a private engagement. As soon as I heard this, I knew that this was the big chance of earning respect that I had been waiting for. The Dalai Lama-—the spiritual leader of Tibetan Buddhism—is one of the most sought-after speakers in the world and can command a fee for one speaking engagement in the six figure range. I knew that it would be a sensation with our members. I immediately pulled off the road to the next public phone and telephoned the number advertised to reserve the Dalai Lama. I secured the Dalai Lama's engagement with a credit card and paid the full fee in advance because I knew that the membership would gladly reimburse me.

My instincts were right. My fellow members were elated that the Dalai Lama would be speaking at our modest gathering, and they immediately voted to reimburse me. The seating arrangements where our society is located in Orange County were made for the event, and I was given the honor of sitting next to our Society's 89-year old sage and spiritual leader, the famous Buddhist Monk, Chuong Chi. You might remember him as the Vietnamese monk who had unsuccessfully tried to immolate himself to protest the War. (The fire never started because Embassy guards covered him with CO_2 foam before he could light the match. Unfortunately, Chuong Chi lost the sight of his left eye as a result of the pressurized foam). Everything was set for the big night, which was scheduled for last Thursday.

It was the happiest moment of my life. In preparation for the Dalai Lama's words, the gathering chanted the Sacred Mantra Summoning Sinless Souls. I couldn't believe it. I was sitting in the front row next to the great Chuong Chi, chanting with him the Sacred Mantra Summoning Sinless Souls! Then, a man who I believed was with the Dalai Lama's entourage, stepped up to the microphone, and said: "Now, without further ado, I give you the sexiest piece of ass this side of Nirvana, the one and only Miss Dolly Lamma!"

To my horror, a buxom redhead sauntered onto the stage. She was dressed completely in leather and began to take off her clothes to the tune of "These Boots Were Made For Walk'n." Near the end of the song, she wore nothing except silver tassels that were (somehow) attached to her nipples. Each tassel strand ended with a sequin. The girl proceeded to gyrate her mammary glands so violently that the tassels whirled like miniature buzz saws, the flashing sequins resembling the teeth of a spinning rotary blade. Then, in an effort to embarrass the old, half-blind Chuong Chi, she bent over the stage to thrust her generous bosom into his face, but a tassel suddenly detached and struck Chuong Chi in his only good eye.

Now, Chuong Chi is totally blind, and he is threatening to sue me for $5,000,000. This amount almost exceeds my entire net worth. He says that he talked to his lawyer and intends to sue me for negligently retaining Miss Dolly Lamma instead of the Dalai Lama.

I'm a realist and I understand that your services will not be cheap. I need the very best representation possible, and I have budgeted $200,000 as a non-refundable flat fee. (I don't like hiring lawyers by the hour because it encourages inefficiency and waste). I realize that sophisticated litigation often costs more than $200,000, but I thought that you might be tempted to take my case if I paid the flat fee up front.

If you believe that I have a case and are willing to represent me as outlined above, please contact me with your thoughts as well as a date and time when we can meet. I look forward to hearing from you.

Very truly yours,

J. Morgan Dumont

Powell, Thompson, Simpson, Gorge & Marks, L.L.P.
Attorneys and Counselors at Law

BENETTE W. POWELL
DONALD J. THOMPSON
ANDREW SIMPSON
ROY P. WALLING
JOEL N. GORGE
JAMES W. MARKS
JENNIFER R. CRANTZ
MARK D. KRAMER
DAVID EAMES

BUILDING

BUFFALO, NEW YORK 14202
TEL: 716.
FAX: 716.
E-MAIL:

WATSON M. KAUFMAN
OF COUNSEL

MASON EMMETT
(1962–1991)

JENNIFER MORRIS
LEGAL ASSISTANT

December 14, 2007

Mr. J. Morgan Dumont, III
9663 Santa Monica Blvd.
Box 274
Beverly Hills, California 90210-4303

Dear Mr. Dumont:

I am afraid that I have a conflict of interest with respect to your matter and cannot take your case. You see, I am already representing a score of injured plaintiffs whose eyes have been put out as a result of those flying sequined tassels worn by strippers. (By the way, those tassels are called "pasties"). I understand that so many of these defective sharp pasties have been placed in commerce that the latest filed cases are being consolidated by the court into a single mass tort litigation.

I agree with you that you are in serious trouble and need an attorney NOW. If I were in your shoes, I would want a lawyer who is already well-educated in both the physics of careening burlesque apparel and the law of products liability specific to pastie design flaws. In order to find such an attorney, I would take the following steps:

(1) Call the Presiding Judge in Orange County, The Honorable C. Robert Jameson. Since this is a vital matter, you should refuse to discuss your case with his secretary or law clerk, and you should insist on speaking only with the Judge himself. If his staff tells you that he is on the bench, make sure that they know it is an emergency warranting the Judge's immediate attention;

(2) Don't be overly formal with the Judge. He hates stodgy, class-conscious people,

and he recoils when litigants and lawyers address him with honorifics such as "Judge" or "Your Honor." He prefers to be addressed as "Robbie" only;

(3) When you speak with Robbie, ask him for the names and addresses of the leading defense lawyers in the "Defective Flying Burlesque Pastie Mass Tort Litigation." He'll immediately know what you're referring to.

(4) During your telephone discussion with Robbie, try not to lisp. He's a good man, but for some reason, he detests people with speech impediments.

Sincerely,

Andrew Simpson

P.S. I know it's you, Bill. Dumont's address is a Mail Boxes Etc., and only a perverted bum like you would have the mind and the time needed to compose that letter!

CHAPTER 5

Mr. Dumont's Patriotic Fantasy Eggs

J. MORGAN DUMONT, III

POST OFFICE BOX 266
HOLICONG, PENNSYLVANIA 18901

January 25, 2010

Blaine B. Quincy, Esq.
Quincy & Brett, P.C.
████████████████
Suite ████████
████████████████
Norristown, PA 19401-████████

CONFIDENTIAL

Dear Ms. Quincy:

I need the help of a commercial lawyer, and a mutual acquaintance has suggested that I contact you. I realize that legal assistance for sophisticated transactions is not cheap, and I am prepared to pay an up front, non-refundable flat fee of $100,000 to the lawyer who I select. I don't want to pay a lawyer by the hour because it encourages inefficiency and waste.

In order for you to help me, I need to give you some background. I am descended from Peter Carl Fabergé, the famous jeweler patronized by the Russian Tsars Alexander III and Nicholas II. Following family tradition, I, too, became a jeweler. I do not waste my time with pedestrian jewelry, but like my great-great-grandfather, I specialize in objects of fantasy.

You are probably familiar with the fabulous Easter eggs that Peter Carl Fabergé designed for the Russian Imperial Court. They were exquisite not only for their intricacy, but they were also dazzlingly inlaid with precious and semi-precious materials. They remain one of the greatest treasures in the history of decorative arts.

I am unlike my great-great grandfather in one critical way — I am an American. Most of us have no appreciation for the unprecedented freedom that we enjoy. I am particularly mindful of our blessings precisely because of the persecution suffered by my family. Peter Carl Fabergé was of Huguenot descent, and his ancestors were arrested, tortured and exiled from France because of their Protestant faith. Peter Carl Fabergé was himself exiled after the Bolshevik coup of 1918, and he was derided by his countrymen as a creator of frivolities and a purveyor of decadence instead of being revered as one of the greatest artists the world has ever known. In 1920, he died in exile at Lausanne, Switzerland, dejected and demoralized.

It is important that you appreciate the foregoing if you are to assist me. I will be celebrating our country, its freedom and blessings by creating a series of fantasy egg masterpieces having patriotic themes. My workshop will be creating 500 fantasy eggs to be sold around the world. Each egg will have an American flag motif and will be set in the finest spinels (red), Australian opals (white) and lapis lazuli (blue). Each American fantasy egg will retail for approximately $35,000.

My studio will also be creating one special fantasy egg to be formally presented to the People of the United States. It will be the most exquisite fantasy egg ever created. Although I am keeping the egg's interior design a secret, I can tell you that the outside will also have the same red, white and blue design, but instead of decorating it with semi-precious stones, I will be using the finest pigeon-blood Burmese rubies (red), cerulean sapphires from Brazil (blue), and colorless diamonds set in platinum (white). The gems have already been selected. They are flawless and perfectly matched. The process of selecting the gems has taken two gemologists five years to accomplish. This gift to the American people is being commissioned anonymously by a billionaire philanthropist and patron of the arts. It will be a national gift befitting the start of a new, more glorious era and the promise of a thousand years of American freedom for the Third Millennium.

We are particularly excited by the prospect of using a new technology called "calcium fossilization" that uses heat and mineral replacement to transform delicate calcite formations into rock-hard semi-translucent stones that have the same qualities of fine white opals. We have successfully used this process to transform common chicken eggs (which are largely comprised of calcium) into iridescent egg-shamed gems. Naturally, however, we will not be using chicken, ostrich or emu eggs that are most often used as fantasy egg decorations. As I am sure you can appreciate, there is only one type of egg that is suitable for my project—authentic eggs of the bald eagle, our national bird and symbol of American might and freedom.

Fortunately for my project, the North American bald eagle was removed from the endangered species list in 1998. It has increased in numbers five-fold since 1974 when DDT was banned. It is now classified only as a "threatened" species under the Endangered Species Act. A lawyer who I consulted advised me that the re-classification of the bald eagle under the Act has important repercussions for my project. Specifically, the regulations promulgated under the Act provide that the nests and eggs of an "endangered" avian species may not be removed, whereas the regulations governing animals that are merely "threatened" do not have a concomitant restriction on egg collection. In other words, I can use real bald eagle eggs which will make my project even more meaningful to Americans. Presently, according to a 1997 wildlife census, there are approximately 1,200 bald eagle nest sites in the lower 48 States. Each female eagle lays one egg per year. Therefore, only a small fraction of the total number of bald eagle eggs need be collected for my project since I plan to use no more than 550 eggs (i.e., 500 plus a 10% breakage allowance).

I am sure that you agree that this is an exciting project, and I hope you feel as proud as I do for being considered to participate by providing legal advice. (My patron is also underwriting the legal fees expended with respect to the donation and sale of these eggs, and he has budgeted $100,000 for legal fees, and he has charged me with taking care of all aspects of this project.)

I need legal advice to protect myself from environmental zealots who might falsely accuse me of having taken bald eagle eggs when they were classified as "endangered" and not merely "threatened." I also need to know the proper legal procedure for making in-kind gifts to the federal government. I understand that it cannot, technically, be a gift to the President of the United States. Does the donation go directly to Congress, or should it go to the Smithsonian Institution. Is there a way for my patron to receive a tax write off for his gift? Also, I need consignment contracts drafted with respect to the fantasy eggs that are to be commercially marketed. (Although jewelers purchase gemstones outright, it is customary in my industry to purchase fantasy decorations on consignment). Finally, I need advice concerning insurance and the risk of loss as to consigned eggs.

I am interviewing one other lawyer, and I am asking both of you to give me your written preliminary thoughts as to how my objectives can best be accomplished as well as your brief analysis of the issues. I will review and compare your replies in determining which lawyer should be retained. Kindly correspond with me promptly.

Very truly yours,

J. Morgan Dumont, III

JMD/km

QUINCY & BRETT, P.C.
ATTORNEYS AT LAW

BLAINE BUNDY QUINCY
RANDOLF T. BRETT

PLACE
SUITE 1█5 █ STREET
NORRISTOWN, PENNSYLVANIA 19401-████

~

TELEPHONE (610) ████████
TELECOPIER (610) ████████
E-mail: ███████@aol.com

February 3, 2010

J. Morgan Dumont, III
P.O. Box 266
Holicong, Pennsylvania 18934-0266

RE: Fantasy Eggs

Dear Mr. Dumont:

Thank you for your letter of introduction and inquiry regarding your Fantasy Egg product. You didn't identify our mutual acquaintance—please send my regards.

I regret that I am unable to respond to your letter. However, please feel free to call my office for an appointment, should you wish to discuss the matter in person.

Very truly yours,

QUINCY & BRETT, P.C.

Blaine Bundy Quincy

BQ/lg

Interview Required
Drop In !!

J. MORGAN DUMONT, III

**POST OFFICE BOX 266
HOLICONG, PENNSYLVANIA 18901**

February 7, 2010

Blaine B. Quincy, Esq.
Quincy & Brett, P.C.
▓▓▓▓▓▓▓▓▓▓▓▓▓▓
Suite ▓▓▓▓
▓▓▓▓▓▓▓▓▓▓▓▓▓▓
Norristown, PA 19401-▓▓▓▓

CONFIDENTIAL

Dear Ms .Quincy:

Thank you for your responsive letter of February 3, 2010. Your suggestion that we meet in person is a great idea. Unless it is inconvenient for you, I will drop in at your office on Thursday, February 22, 2010, at 10:00 A.M.

In order to get you up to speed on the bald eagle egg collection aspect of my project, I think you should watch a video that was prepared by Raptor Trophies, Inc. Raptor Trophies is a foreign-based company that acts as a hunting guide for sportsmen and as a procurement company for the Chinese medicine market. (Eagle and hawk talons and livers command a high price in the Orient. I will fast-forward through the parts of the presentation concerning the harvesting of golden eagles, hawks and other non-endangered birds of prey.) Unfortunately, the video is in Russian, so I will have to come with a translator.

The video shows how the bald eagles are tracked and how their nests are located. It also shows the great care taken by Raptor Trophies in collecting the eggs. I think you'll be impressed by the video, and it will assuage fears of any reasonable person that eggs are being recklessly exploited. Anticipating that you will have neither a television nor a DVD player in your office, I will provide both.

I look forward to meeting you.

Very truly yours,

J. Morgan Dumont

J. Morgan Dumont

P.S. Barbara (the Opera Guild) sends her best regards.

QUINCY & BRETT, P.C.

ATTORNEYS AT LAW

BLAINE BUNDY QUINCY
RANDOLF T. BRETT

PLACE
SUITE 105 ████████████ STREET
NORRISTOWN, PENNSYLVANIA 19401-████

~

TELEPHONE (610) ████████
TELECOPIER (610) ████████
E-mail: █████@aol.com

February 11, 2010

J. Morgan Dumont, III
P.O. Box 266
Holicong, Pennsylvania 18934-0266

Dear Mr. Dumont:

Thank you for your letter of February 7, 2010. Without a last name, I am unable to identify the "Barbara" of the Opera Guild, to whom you refer.

Barring sudden emergency, February 22, 2010 at 10:00 a.m. is convenient for an office meeting. However, before we meet, I do want to advise you of our billing practices and method of legal representation. A sample representation form is enclosed for your review.

Due to the complex and diverse nature of your project, I would not provide an opinion letter without conducting research. My hourly rate is $200.00. Costs are invoiced separately. A retainer of at least $15,000.00 would be required to initiate research. Any unused portion of the retainer would be refundable.

I must state unequivocally that until the research portion would be completed and an opinion letter presented, I am in no position to comment on the viability of your project, or to whether the information you have already provided is accurate.

Very truly yours,

QUINCY & BRETT, P.C.

Blaine Bundy Quincy

BQ/lg
enclosure

Raptor trophies
a russian mercenary legion company

SEND REPLY CORRESPONDENCE TO
NIGERIAN DROP BOX:
Raptor Trophies
PMB 3962
Port Harcourt
Rivers State Nigeria

15. Feb. 2010

B. Quincy
Quincy & Brett

Norristown, PA 19401

Dear Quincy:

You may call me Val. I work for company hired by client of yours [Mr. D] that want us to get special eggs for him. Mr. D want dvd film of bird of pray egg hunt to run in office on 22 Feb 2010 at 1000 hours. Will take television and dvd to office. Be there on time. Make sure you got blinds or curtains for privacy. You, me and Mr. D only be there. Send secretary out for coffee or something. No cops.

Val

QUINCY & BRETT, P.C.

ATTORNEYS AT LAW

BLAINE BUNDY QUINCY
RANDOLF T. BRETT

████████ PLACE
SUITE 1██ ████████ STREET
NORRISTOWN, PENNSYLVANIA 19401-████

~

TELEPHONE (610) ████████
TELECOPIER (610) ████████
E-mail: ████@aol.com

February 16, 2010

J. Morgan Dumont, III
P. O. Box 266
Holicong, Pennsylvania 189328-0266

Re: Fantasy Eggs

Dear Mr. Dumont:

After discussing this matter with my partner, we have decided that we are not the right law firm for your fantasy egg project. We feel that your enterprise requires analysis of federal and state criminal laws, and we are not criminal lawyers. I suggest that you retain a law firm that has the capability of providing both civil and criminal advice that you will need. Accordingly, we will be canceling our appointment for February 22, 2010.

Since we cannot take your case, please make sure that you inform your contact at Raptor Trophies not come to our office on February 22, especially since my partner and I have scheduled appointments out of the office that day. Thank you for your interest in our firm, and best of luck to you.

Very truly yours,

QUINCY & BRETT, P.C.

Blaine Bundy Quincy

BQ/lg
enclosure

CHAPTER 6

Mr. Dumont's Dermatological Revolution

J. MORGAN DUMONT, III

POST OFFICE BOX 266
HOLICONG, PENNSYLVANIA 18901

January 28, 2010

Terrance R. Jameson, Esq.
Santagota & Jameson
██████████████████
Huntingdon Valley, Pennsylvania 19006

CONFIDENTIAL

Dear Mr. Jameson:

I need the help of a commercial lawyer to launch a new product, and a mutual acquaintance has suggested that I contact you. I realize that sophisticated legal counsel is not cheap, and I am prepared to pay an up front, non-refundable flat fee of $150,000 to the lawyer who I select. I don't like paying lawyers by the hour because it encourages inefficiency and waste.

I belong to one of the richest families in America. Contrary to what you might think, this has been a curse, not a blessing. I say this because having a superabundance of everything stifles ambition. As a result, I did not take school seriously, and I barely graduated from college. I briefly attended medical school (thanks to a seven-figure gift from my Grandmother). Because I am artistically inclined, my goal was to become a reconstructive plastic surgeon. Unfortunately, I didn't pay attention to my studies, and in my third year of medical school, I was asked to leave.

Nevertheless, I continued my interest in medicine, and I worked in several research laboratories for drug manufacturers on projects related to medicinal cosmetics. Please don't confuse medicinal cosmetics with vanity products that are designed to camouflage skin defects. The cosmetic products that I have tried to develop are systemic drugs that alter skin growth, hair loss, varicose vein development, muscle tone and retardation of scar tissue formation. For the last 21 years, I've worked in the labs of two pharmaceutical giants. Three years ago, I decided to use my family wealth to form a new venture so that I would have creative freedom to develop medical cosmetics.

I opened up my own independent laboratory, and I have hired some of the most talented chemists and medical research personnel in the industry. At first, we worked on a promising lead on ameliorating the symptoms of telangiectasia (a condition that manifests itself in the visible dilation of skin blood vessels). However, we eventually abandoned that project because the drug that we developed proved to increase blood pressure in laboratory animals. My new company lost several million dollars pursuing this dead end. Next, one of our researchers came up with a lead with respect to treatment of the visible symptoms of a serious internal disorder that affects the skin known as systemic sclerosis. This disease causes hardening of the skin known as "scleroderma" due to an increase in the connective tissue of the dermis and marked tethering of the dermal connective tissue to subcutaneous tissues. We believed that the condition caused skin fibroblasts to produce excessive amounts of collagen. However, the drug that we developed caused the complete cessation of collagen production, which would have ultimately destroyed the elastic properties of the patient's skin. Again, the company lost several more millions on this R&D project, and my startup enterprise was in danger of foundering.

I was desperate. We re-examined our old research to determine whether there was any way in which to salvage the project. Just when we were beginning to give up hope, we came across some lab results that had originally been ignored as being irrelevant. One of the chemical components that we developed for our drug had a peculiar effect on certain specialized muscles. Fortunately, the efficacious ingredient in the compound need not be synthesized but can be extracted from a widely available tropical plant that has already been approved for a non-prescription use. In other words, FDA approval would not be necessary. In laboratory animals, the drug expands certain types of specialized muscles without causing any side effects. Thereafter, we investigated whether our discovery had any commercial application.

We were initially disappointed to learn that, as to human beings, there is only one muscle that responds to our chemical compound—the dartos fascia. The dartos is the smooth muscle tissue that lies immediately under the skin of the scrotum. Its purpose is to expand or relax the scrotal wall in order to regulate the temperature of the testes. When my compound is topically applied as a cream, the dartos expands to its maximum size, and the scrotum becomes absolutely smooth and has a full, rounded look.

Probably like you, my initial reaction was, "So what?" Again, I thought I was at a dead end. However, one night after dinner, I was bathing my little boy, and my 11 year old daughter came into the bathroom. She asked, "Daddy, what's that thing hanging under Timmy's wienie." I told her that it was Timmy's scrotum, and she immediately responded, "I'm glad I don't have one cause it looks so oogie." I laughed, and told my wife what my daughter said. She laughed, too, but quickly added that, to women young and old, scrotums are "oogie." She said that practically every girl would agree that the scrotum is ugly when it takes on its wrinkled, corrugated look (i.e., when the dartos relaxes).

In order to keep my business afloat, I decided to market this compound as a topical cosmetic cream to be rubbed onto the scrotum. I know that at first glance it appears absurd, but the more that I thought about it, I convinced myself that there is a huge dormant market for my product. Most men would be upset if their faces became corrugated and wrinkled, so why should they tolerate wrinkles on their scrotums? After all, whether in the bedroom or in a bathing suit, many men would no doubt prefer to sport a well-rounded, full scrotum.

After further research, we discovered that our topical anti-wrinkle scrotum cream would have tremendous marketing potential in connection with the tattoo industry. Several tattoo operators have told me that my new anti-wrinkle scrotum cream will sell so quickly that their biggest concern is whether we can keep our supply in pace with their demand. The tattooing of private parts is all the rage in certain segments of our society. However, permanent pictographs are rarely applied to the scrotum. The reason might surprise you. It is not that the scrotum is too sensitive to be pricked by tattoo needles. Scrotums are rarely tattooed because the wrinkles, folds and corrugated appearance of a relaxed genital sac make it difficult to discern the artwork. In fact, an owner of one tattoo parlor told me about his only experience at tattooing a scrotum. He said that one customer constantly bragged about having a "nuclear sex drive." In keeping with this description of his libido, he asked the tattoo artist to depict an atomic bomb blast on his scrotum. When the scrotum was in its full expanse, the tattoo had its desired effect, but when the scrotum relaxed, it looked like a shriveled button mushroom.

We are about to begin production, and we have already developed our marketing approach. The product's slogan will be, "Don't put your family jewels in a wrinkled sac!" (We decided that a humorous approach to our product would work best). Moreover, our anti-wrinkle scrotum cream will be available in depilatory or non-depilatory form. The cream without the depilatory will be marketed under the name, "SmoothBalls" and the scrotum cream with the depilatory will be sold under the brand name "CueBalls".

I need products liability advice concerning warnings and disclaimers. Should my product be marketed by a subsidiary corporation? What about advertising issues? Does the fact that that the cream is applied to the male genitalia in any way limit our rights to advertise in family magazines? I also need legal counsel in order to prepare requirements contracts with the suppliers of the tropical plants from which the active ingredient in our product is extracted. I will also need form contracts prepared between our company and wholesalers and retailers.

I am prepared to pay the above-described fee and a bonus if my objectives are accomplished. I am interviewing one other lawyer, and I am asking both of you to give me your written preliminary thoughts as to how my objectives can best be accomplished as well as your brief analysis of the issues. I will review and compare your replies in determining which lawyer should be retained. Kindly correspond with me promptly.

Very truly yours,

J. Morgan Dumont

J. Morgan Dumont, III

JMD/km

SANTAGOTA & JAMESON, P.C.
ATTORNEYS AT LAW

Kenneth J. Santagota★★
Terrance R. Jameson

★★*Also Member of the NJ and FLA Bars*

T▓▓▓▓▓▓▓▓▓▓▓
2▓▓▓▓▓▓ Pike
Huntingdon Valley, Pennsylvania 19006
215-▓▓▓▓▓
Fax 215-▓▓▓▓▓▓

Of Counsel:
Kenneth J. Santagota
Samuel Barker

February 15, 2010

J. Morgan Dumont, III
P. O. Box 266
Holicong, Pennsylvania 18928-0266

Legal work concerning your new project

Dear Mr. Dumont:

Thank you for your letter of January 28, 2010. 1 began to prepare a formal response to your letter, taking into consideration the legal issues which you will encounter to market your product as well as the legal structure that should surround your enterprise. In drafting said response, it was clear that I would require considerable more information about you, your product and your proposed enterprise. I believe that we would both be served well by a face-to-face meeting wherein I could ascertain information about your enterprise.

I know that I could be of unique legal assistance to your enterprise as I have represented many large companies with regard to new and unique initiatives such as taking products overseas when I worked in Washington, D.C. for the law firm of Baker & McKenzie, which is the largest law firm in the world. With my present practice, I am able to bring that same sophisticated legal assistance for small to medium-sized businesses.

Please contact me, at your earliest convenience in order to determine a time and place to meet to discuss your venture.

Best Regards

Terrance R. Jameson

Great!!
Hire this lawyer →

J. MORGAN DUMONT, III

POST OFFICE BOX 266
HOLICONG, PENNSYLVANIA 18901

February 19, 2010

Terrance R. Jameson, Esq.
Santagota & Jameson
█████████████████

Huntingdon Valley, Pennsylvania 19006

CONFIDENTIAL

     Re: Anti-Wrinkle Scrotum Cream

Dear Mr. Jameson:

Thank you for your reply letter of February 15, 2010. I was impressed by your top-flight credentials. When I read that you got your legal training at the largest law firm in the world, I immediately concluded that you are probably the right lawyer to assist me with the legal hurdles relating to the manufacturing and marketing of my anti-wrinkle scrotum cream.

I agree with you that a personal meeting is best. Therefore, unless it is inconvenient for you, I'll drop in at your office on March 6, 2010, at 3:00 P.M.

The first issue that I want you to address at our meeting concerns the TV infomercial that we have produced to market our anti-wrinkle scrotum cream. The half-hour infomercial deals with all facets of our scrotum cream, and it might stimulate thinking as to potential issues that we haven't yet spotted.

Our infomercial features 16 well-endowed men who give "before and after" demonstrations of how our anti-wrinkle scrotum cream works. (Obviously, because of male frontal nudity, we have to air our infomercial solely on cable). It shows application of the cream on their genitals in front of a live (paid) audience. I admit that it's a little hoakie, but the paid audience oohs, aahs and applauds on cue when the scrotums expand on camera to their maximum circumference. (Our advertising people insisted on this approach). Both before and after the application of our cream, our models wear thong swimwear in order to show how much sexier a guy is when his genitals are amply swollen.

The infomercial also shows how the cream's effect persists even when genitals become sweat-soaked. It features our nude models playing beach volleyball, and close-up shots of each of our jumping athletes reveal how our cream lingers to ensure the maintenance of a well-rounded scrotum. Finally, the infomercial shows a tattoo artist at work decorating a genital sac. When you see the infomercial, I'm sure you'll agree that the effectiveness of the pictograph after the anti-wrinkle scrotum cream is applied is stunning.

When I come for our meeting, we can watch the infomercial together and discuss it. Also, please advise as to whether you would like a sample tin of anti-wrinkle scrotum cream, compliments of my company. If so, please specify whether you would like "Soothballs" or our cream with the depilatory, "Cueballs." I look forward to meeting you.

Very truly yours,

J. Morgan Dumont

SANTAGOTA & JAMESON, P.C.
ATTORNEYS AT LAW

Kenneth J. Santagota**
Terrance R. Jameson

**Also Member of the NJ and FLA Bars

T█████████████████

2█████████ Pike

Huntingdon Valley, Pennsylvania 19006

215-█████████

Fax 215-█████████

Of Counsel:
Kenneth J. Santagota
Samuel Barker

February 25, 2010

J. Morgan Dumont, III
P.O. Box 266
Holicong, Pennsylvania 18928-0266

Dear Mr. Dumont:

I received your letter of February 19, 2010, in which you propose to show a dvd video presentation of your product. In reviewing this matter with my partner, we have concluded that we do not possess the resources to effectuate your business objectives. On further reflection, we now think that it would be best for you to retain an attorney who specializes in FDA matters, since your product might be subject to administrative regulations—an area in which we unfortunately do not specialize.

Best Regards,

Terrance R. Jameson

*Just playing
hard to get
Follow up letter
Required*

J. MORGAN DUMONT, III

POST OFFICE BOX 266
HOLICONG, PENNSYLVANIA 18901

March 2, 2010

Terrance R. Jameson, Esq.
Santagota & Jameson
████████████████
Huntingdon Valley, Pennsylvania 19006

CONFIDENTIAL

   Re: Anti-Wrinkle Scrotum Cream

Dear Mr. Jameson:

   When I received your last letter of February 25, I realized that I might have offended you by assuming that you would have a video entertainment system in your office on which you would be able to view my "Smoothballs" presentation. I realize now that it was stupid of me to assume that serious lawyers would have TV's and DVD players in their offices, and I apologize for suggesting, albeit unintentionally, that you are not a true professional. Please accept my apology.

   Now that this misunderstanding is out of the way, I want to resume our lawyer/client relationship. When I visit you on March 6 as originally planned, I won't bring my "Smoothballs" DVD video for reasons already mentioned. Instead, I'll bring a sample which I can apply at the office so that you can see its amazing results. I'll bring latex gloves with me since without your seeing the video presentation, you won't know the precise way to massage the cream onto the scrotum.

   By the way, the FDA issues have already been addressed during the development stage, so there is no need to refer this matter out. Be assured, however that I appreciate your willingness to put my need to obtain the best representation above your own financial interest. I was very impressed. See you soon!

Very truly yours,

J. Morgan Dumont

J. Morgan Dumont, III

NO REPLY!

JMD:km

GEORGE G. STOLTZ
Attorney at Law

Telephone: (305) ██████	████████████ **Blvd.**
Fascimile: (305) ██████	**Suite** ██████
E-Mail: ████████**/@prodigy.net**	**Coral Gables, FL 33134**

January 18, 2010

Mr. J. Morgan Dumont, III
6901 W. Okeechobee Blvd., D5
Box 161
West Palm Beach, FL 33411

Re: Your letter dated December 30, 2009

Dear Mr. Dumont:

I am in receipt of your letter dated December 30, 2009. Before I can consider representing you or your company, I will need to know some further details. Whenever I take on a new client, I find it best to know exactly how they learned about me. Please tell me the name of the mutual acquaintance who suggested you contact me. Also, would you please tell me the name of your company, if any, names and addresses of all other investors individually and corporately, including the names of your board of directors and officers, which will enable me to properly check for potential conflicts of interest.

Both your letter and your product are somewhat unusual. In reviewing your letter, I am somewhat at a loss regarding how long you want us to act as your outside general counsel. For example, if your proposed $150,000 fee is intended to cover a period of years of work, it is too little. Accordingly, we will need to discuss the duration of our professional services as your general counsel.

If you want to proceed, please telephone my office at your earliest convenience for an appointment. I look forward to meeting you.

Interview Required
Drop In !!

Sincerely,

~~████████████~~

George G. Stoltz

GGS:nt

J. MORGAN DUMONT, III

POST OFFICE BOX 192
MECHANICSVILLE, PENNSYLVANIA 18934-0192

January 27, 2010

George G. Stoltz, Esq.
██████████████████
Coral Gables, Florida 33134

CONFIDENTIAL

Dear Mr. Stoltz:

I am in receipt of your reply letter concerning my anti-wrinkle scrotum cream and my company, Softballs Unlimited. Thank you. All of the issues that you raised in your correspondence are best addressed person to person. To that end, I will drop in at your office on March 8, 2010, at 4:00 P.M.

Softballs is looking for professionals to endorse our anti-wrinkle scrotum cream, (e.g., doctors, lawyers, soldiers, athletes, etc.) We anticipate that the endorsement will benefit the professional endorser by giving him free nation-wide advertising. In keeping with our company's slogan (about not keeping the family jewels in a wrinkled sac), each endorsement will have a humorous theme. As part of your compensation package, would you be willing to give a professional endorsement? Our advertising people would like an attorney endorsement on the package to this effect:

In the court room, he has brass balls,
But in the bedroom, they turn to "SmoothBalls."

Before you make up your mind on this issue, I would appreciate it if you would try our product. You seem receptive to getting all the facts, so I thought that I'd bring tins of "SmoothBalls" and "Cueballs" to our meeting. (Of course, you don't have to apply it in front of me). Think about it.

I look forward to meeting you.

Very truly yours,

J. Morgan Dumont

J. Morgan Dumont, III

GEORGE G. STOLTZ
Attorney at Law

Telephone: (305) ██████
Fascimile: (305) ██████
E-Mail: ██████@prodigy.net

██████ Blvd.
Suite ██████
Coral Gables, FL 33134

March 2, 2010

Mr. J. Morgan Dumont, III
6901 W. Okeechobee Blvd., D5
Box 161
West Palm Beach, FL 33411

Re: Your letter of February 24, 2010

Dear Mr. Dumont:

In your last letter, you stated that you would be dropping in to see me on March 8 at 4:00 p.m. I will not be in the office that day, so please telephone as soon as possible in order to reschedule. When we meet, I will want to inspect your product, but I won't need to sample it for myself.

I don't think it would be a good idea to have me act as both your attorney and your product promoter, but thank you for your offer. Besides, I am a corporate lawyer, not a litigator, so your slogan about me having brass ones in the courtroom really wouldn't fit.

I look forward to hearing from you soon.

Sincerely,

George G. Stoltz

GGS:nt

CHAPTER 7

Mr. Dumont's Employment Opportunity for the Disadvantaged

CONFIDENTIAL

J. MORGAN DUMONT, III

104 W. CHESTNUT STREET, BOX 219
HINSDALE, ILLINOIS 60521-3387

December 30, 2009

Frederick B. Figge, Esq.

████████████████

Aurora, Illinois 60506 ████████

CONFIDENTIAL

Dear Mr. Figge:

A mutual acquaintance has given me your name. I need the help of a commercial lawyer to assist me with a startup enterprise that promises to be incredibly lucrative. I don't like paying professionals by the hour. Please don't be offended, but paying lawyers for their time is stupid. It is a system by which the most inefficient lawyers are financially rewarded. Instead of remunerating you on an hourly basis, I propose to pay a $350,000 flat fee to the lawyer who I select for all work performed. As an incentive, I will agree that this $350,000 be up front and non-refundable.

The following background is necessary for you to assist me. I am independently wealthy, and it has been my privilege to have enjoyed abundant leisure time. As a young man, I learned that too much leisure is boring and demoralizing, eventually leading one to lament the purposelessness of life. Accordingly, 36 years ago, I developed a hobby that became my life's passion—antique time keeping. I have become known as one of the world's leading experts on one specialized type of time piece called a chronometer that was used by mariners to calculate their longitudinal position.

The first chronometers that were manufactured during the reign of King George III are still among the most intricate, fine and complex mechanisms that mankind has ever devised. They are crammed with the tiniest imaginable gears, jewels and springs. Each of the hundreds of components are interrelated and interactive. Because they had to function on ships, they were built to be accurate regardless of changing temperature, humidity, salinity, and acidity. These two hundred year-old chronometers kept precise time even if the ship on which they were placed constantly pitched, yawled and rolled.

Chronometers are, in effect, ultra-precision watches. However, unlike watches, they contain helical balance springs, spring detents, fusees, pivots, gimbals and compensation balance mechanisms. These tiny devices work together to provide constant torque to the mainspring, which causes the chronometer to remain accurate to .1 seconds per day even on the high seas. Until 30 years ago, mechanical chronometers were still being made that were remarkably small--approximately double the size of the average pocket watch.

Mechanical chronometers are still made today, but, believe it or not, chronometers can no longer be made as small as they had been several centuries ago. The reason for this might surprise you. It's not that the old chronometers are too complicated to understand or that we have lost the technology to reproduce their components. Instead, they cannot be duplicated because the only lubricant in the world that is suitable to the long-term maintenance of compact chronometers is no longer available. That lubricant was sperm whale oil.

Crude sperm whale oil is a wax that is contained in the massive cranial cavities of the sperm whale. (Experts in marine mammals have theorized that this wax protects the whale's internal organs from pressure when it hunts squid at great depths). This oil is not to be confused with the lamp oil that was extracted from the mammal's blubber by boiling it. Before whaling was banned, the oil was subjected to a complicated refining process. The end result was sperm whale lubricant oil, which was, and has always been, unsurpassed as a lubricant for high-speed machinery and precision instruments such as chronometers. Notwithstanding advances in modern chemistry, the unique properties of sperm whale lubricant oil have not been synthesized.

If such a lubricant could be synthesized, it would, of course, be a boon to chronometer hobbyists like me, but it would have a tremendous impact in industries in which miniature/micro precision machinery is used. For example, I understand that the aerospace industry would be eager for such a lubricant because it would dramatically extend the life of critical machine parts. This translates to fewer in-flight failures and the saving of human life. The person who finds an equivalent to sperm lubricating oil stands to make a fortune, and such a discovery would, undoubtedly, reduce future pressures to harvest sperm whales.

I have discovered a substitute for sperm whale lubricating oil! In fact, the viscosity and co-efficient of friction of this substitute are both lower than that of sperm whale lubricant oil, and (remarkably), it is even more buoyant. Moreover, it is a natural, not a synthetic, substance. I discovered it through serendipity.

Please forgive me if the following is unpleasant, but you need to know the nature of my discovery in order for you to assist me. Last year, I was sick with a rare parasitical inflammation of the small intestine. It caused horrific abdominal pain, and it made me so sick that I vomited constantly. Moreover, when I went to the bathroom, my feces were nauseatingly odiferous. Not only was their stench unbelievable, it was impossible to flush them after a bowel movement. As a result, I was forced to scoop the floating stools out of the toilet and bury them in my backyard.

The inflammation caused my gallbladder to produce enormous quantities of high cholesterol bile on which the parasite thrived. The parasite metabolized my bile and excreted a by-product of that process. This by-product was the substance that had saturated my stools and made them super-buoyant.

After I was successfully treated with sulfur tablets that killed the intestinal parasites, it occurred to me that the substance that had saturated my feces must have possessed unusual buoyancy characteristics. I dug up my stools, and to my astonishment, they remained as moist and slippery as they were on the day on which I had excreted them. Later, I pressed the excrement and filtered the oil therefrom to produce the finest lubricating oil on earth.

My idea is this. I can get minorities from the ghettos to ingest the parasite. They could then collect the lubricating oil that the resulting illness creates. It would be a perfect job for them. The parasite is not affected by narcotics or alcohol, and, because the infection renders one bedridden, it wouldn't impinge on their life style since they don't work anyway. They would simply be required to collect their stools and hang them from cheesecloth bags at room temperature. A beaker (supplied by me at no cost) would be placed to catch the oil that drips from the hung cheesecloth bags. Once they produced a certain agreed-upon quantity of oil, I would then pay for the sulfur treatments for the eradication of their parasites. It's a great opportunity for their kind. I would pay them two to three times more than they could get by staying on welfare, i.e., $22,000 per year. Not bad for a job whose only effort is to hang feces in a bag.

After further refinement, I am sure that my oil will command prices that exceed the current cost of the next-best specialized lubricant-- $43 per ml. I estimate that an average adult host for the parasite would produce 2.3 liters of oil in six months i.e., $98,900 worth of oil. I would pay the host approximately $11,000 for just six months of his services. You can see that the profit potential is incredible.

I have several problems to work out. Just like crossing the street, there's a risk. Specifically, there is a small (3.8 percent) mortality rate associated with this parasitical infection. I need to make sure that the contracts I use contain an unassailable disclosure and waiver form that makes clear that my suppliers have assumed the risk. What about the FDA? How about the EPA (hazardous medical wastes?)

I am interviewing one other lawyer, and I am asking both of you to give me your written preliminary thoughts as to what litigation strategy you would employ as well as your brief analysis of the issues. I will review and compare your replies in determining which lawyer should be retained. Kindly correspond with me promptly.

Very truly yours,

J. Morgan Dumont

J. Morgan Dumont, III

FREDERICK B. FIGGE
ATTORNEY AT LAW
████████ BLVD.
AURORA, ILLINOIS 60506-3854

PHONE: (630) ████
FAX: (630) ████

January 6, 2010

J. Morgan Dumont, III
104 W. Chestnut Street
P. O. Box 219
Hillsdale, Illinois 60521-3387

Re: Solicitation Letter of December 30, 2009

Dear Mr. Dumont:

Your unconventional letter requires a like reply.

The commercial idea proposed in that letter is not practical because it hits certain profound legal, ethical, and social issues. Although I understand your reluctance to want to pay hourly rates, Abraham Lincoln noted that all a lawyer can sell is time, so I will briefly lay out the reasons for this preliminary assessment.

1. I cannot conceive of any legitimate way a governmental authority would approve of what amounts to the deliberate infection of otherwise healthy people with something that is potentially deadly purely for the production of a commercial product. I'll concede historical problems with tobacco and alcohol in this sphere, but the tide certainly is running the wrong way on trying to use those as precedents for a new invention today.

2. The biological and medical natures of the product mean far more than just EPA requirements. Add the FDA, Center for Disease Control, National Institutes for Health, etc.

3. Because of the previous reasons, liability insurance isn't a likely possibility so that the business will be a self-insurer. Criminal and civil personal liability of business principals is a big risk.

4. You are seeking an unassailable liability release. I can't provide that and would question anyone who would say such a document exists. You can get a good one, a strong one, but not one that can assuredly defeat any claim, no matter the facts, in perpetuity. After nearly twenty years of practice, I realize that crafting a perfect anything in law is as futile as looking for a unicorn. The best I can do is improve on what's been done before, be perceptive enough to point out where potential flaws may exist (so my client can weigh the risks too), and move on.

5. Any endeavor to exploit this product would require medical supervision and input. The manner of production almost certainly runs up against the Hippocratic Oath.

6. I'd hate to defend to the media, authorities, and almost any advocacy organization other than the Klan and its relatives the population targeted for recruitment as "producers".

7. This proposal needs a paradigm shift from its focus on humans as industrial processes. Think bio-engineering and technical development. Legal work on employment, supply, and development contracts, patents or trade secrets, and other professionally challenging subjects would still be required.

If my reply indicates I combine the insight, experience, independence, and character you desire, please contact me to schedule a mutually convenient meeting. Please be forewarned that I don't have staff, although I have voicemail, and do need some advance notice to arrange my calendar.

Very truly yours,

Frederick B. Figge

Great!!
Hire this lawyer!!

J. MORGAN DUMONT, III

104 W. CHESTNUT STREET, BOX 219
HINSDALE, ILLINOIS 60521-3387

January 26, 2010

Frederick B. Figge, Esq.

▓▓▓▓▓▓▓▓▓▓▓

Aurora, Illinois 60506-▓▓▓▓

CONFIDENTIAL

Dear Mr. Figge:

I greatly appreciated you letter of January 6, 2010, which has taken a few weeks for me to digest. It really was an eye-opener for me. I agree with your assessment. I need to pursue production in a country where libertarianism is taken seriously, where paternalistic government doesn't prohibit its citizens from taking personal risks and where the disadvantaged who strive to create wealth have a decent chance of succeeding.

What if my producers came from Third-World countries? Wouldn't that eliminate most of these legalistic obstacles? I think it's time for me to come in for a consultation so that we can begin working out the details. Please pick any date and time during February, and I'll be there.

By the way, I think that the reference to the Klan was unfair. Since when has the Klan been at all interested in helping Coloreds achieve economic parity with Whites? In any event, onward and upwards!

Very truly yours,

J. Morgan Dumont

J. Morgan Dumont

FREDERICK B. FIGGE
ATTORNEY AT LAW
████████ BLVD.
AURORA, ILLINOIS 60506-3854

PHONE: (630)████
FAX: (630)████

February 7, 2010

J. Morgan Dumont, III
104 W. Chestnut Street
P. O. Box 219
Hillsdale, Illinois 60521-3387

Dear Mr. Dumont:

I don't believe that your proposal to circumvent U.S. safety laws by using Third World hosts for the parasite will insulate you from criminal responsibility imposed by our judicial system. Even more to the point, your modified proposal does nothing to address the moral problems associated with infecting persons with potentially deadly organisms simply so you can make a profit.

I am sorry but I cannot agree to represent you if you are determined to use human "producers" for your new lubricant. However, if you are willing to pursue your project by finding some means of production that does not involve the purposeful infection of human beings, I would be happy to assist you in all aspects of your enterprise. If you want to proceed with some alternative production proposal, please contact my office for a consultation.

Very truly yours,

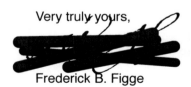

Frederick B. Figge

J. MORGAN DUMONT, III

104 W. CHESTNUT STREET, BOX 219
HINSDALE, ILLINOIS 60521-3387

February 12, 2010

Frederick B. Figge, Esq.
██████████████

Aurora, Illinois 60506-████

CONFIDENTIAL

Dear Mr. Figge:

Your letter of February 7, 2010, confirms my initial suspicion that you harbor racist attitudes toward minorities in our country and people of color around the world. I have devised a plan by which the poor can lift themselves by their bootstraps and proudly earn a decent wage instead of "living on the dole." Your reluctance to advance my objective in this regard leads me to the inescapable conclusion that you are a closet white supremist bent on denying minorities the right to realize the American dream. You make me sick.

Very truly yours,

J. Morgan Dumont

J. Morgan Dumont

NO REPLY!

CHAPTER 8

Mr. Dumont's Number One Son

J. MORGAN DUMONT, III

9663 SANTA MONICA BLVD., BOX 274
BEVERLY HILLS, CALIFORNIA 90210-4303

January 3, 2010

Michael David Price, Esq.

Suite

Los Angeles, CA 90025

CONFIDENTIAL

Dear Mr. Price:

A mutual acquaintance has urged me to contact you. I need the help of a lawyer for a trust fund that I want to establish. I realize that sophisticated legal counsel is not cheap, and I am prepared to pay an up front, non-refundable flat fee of $75,000 to the lawyer who I select. I don't like paying lawyers by the hour because it encourages inefficiency and waste.

I am in the entertainment business, and it's possible that you might have heard of the act that I manage, "Finclops, The Incredible One-Eyed Merman." "Finclops" is actually my 13 year old son, Phineas Dumont. He suffers from two unusual physical malformations. In other words, Phineas is, for lack of a better word, a freak—a term that Phineas and his family accept without shame or remorse. You see, Phineas is also my treasure, and much beloved by his family. (Of course, the bit about him being a Merman is obviously showman's hype). Forgive me if you already know about the science of teratology (the study of biological malformations), but I need to tell you the following if you are to help me.

Teratologists around the world have fought for the opportunity to examine Phineas because he is one of the most unusual freaks ever recorded. He was born with (what teratologists call) "grotesque" congenital defects. First, he has the most prominent cyclopean malformation seen in the Twentieth Century. You might have seen an anophthalmiac, i.e., an eyeless person. They draw big money at carnival midways. However, Phineas has a much more rare malformation. He has a single eye almost directly above the bridge of his nose. It's really a startling effect. If it weren't for his small stature, Phineas would look just like the fabled Cyclops of Homer's Odyssey. For this reason alone, the kid is an amazing carnival draw.

Phineas was born with another bizarre malformation. He is a sirenoid. Specifically, instead of being born with two legs and two feet, he has a sirenomeulus. A sirenomeulus is a single fused limb with no feet. Sirenoids should not to be confused with the more pedestrian freak, a skiapod (one-legged person). For obvious reasons, the name of the condition is derived from the mythical creature, the siren or mermaid. Hence, Phineas' show name, "Finclops, The Incredible One-Eyed Merman." I realize that it might sound cheesy to you, but at carnival midway shows, Phineas wears a flesh-toned flipper on the end of his sirenomeulus. When working his act, Phineas is absolutely naked (except for the flipper), and you would be stunned by the number of apparently intelligent people who, after seeing him, are convinced that he is an actual one-eyed merman!

His mother and I felt cursed the day he was born. I mean, we knew plenty of other parents who regularly dropped LSD and didn't get a freak out of the deal. However, in retrospect, Phineas' malformations have been a blessing in disguise. As you can imagine, Phineas is a gold mine. For example, last summer at the Texas State Fair, Phineas drew an average of $31,000 per day over six days. I book his act with all the major carnivals and state fairs throughout the nation, and we do particularly well in foreign countries where a quality freak show is still appreciated. Phineas has made me a millionaire many times over. I admit that I have been a little lax in the past when it comes to accounting matters, and I thought that I should appease the child welfare butt-ins by making some separate formal arrangement by which Phineas would formally share in the profits of the act.

My current handshake deal with Phineas is as follows: As manager, promoter, agent, bookkeeper and caretaker, I get 85% of the take, and Phineas gets the other 15%. In case you think this is greedy, keep in mind that I house, feed and (at least when he's not performing) clothe Phineas out of my share of the profits. Even more importantly, I pay for the boy's medical exams and doctor's bills, which typically run about 30% more than medical care for a normal kid! Believe me, it's a real drain on my savings account. Still, I'm willing to give up some of my share for the purpose of creating a trust account for Phineas' benefit.

What I want you to do is set up a trust account in which I will pay 25% of the profits into a trust account for Phineas. I will be the trustee. Of course, if I'm giving up an additional 10% of my share of the profits in order to create this trust, I want all of Phineas' needs to be paid from the trust account, not from my share of the profits.

Furthermore, as trustee, I want the liberal right to invade corpus for any purpose that I deem necessary or desirable for the boy's welfare.

By the way, can we structure the trust so that Phineas pays the mortgage payments on the family vacation home in Palm Beach as a kind of rental payment to me? After all, during the off season, Phineas has been able to enjoy our beach home even though he hasn't paid me a dime, and it only seems fair to me that he should carry his load.

I am interviewing one other lawyer, and I am asking both of you to give me your written preliminary thoughts as to how my objectives can best be accomplished as well as your brief analysis of the issues. I will review and compare your replies in determining which lawyer should be retained. Kindly correspond with me promptly.

Very truly yours,

Morgan Dumont, III

JMD/km

LAW OFFICES OF

MICHAEL DAVID PRICE

████████ BOULEVARD
SUITE █████
LOS ANGELES, CALIFORNIA 90025
TELEPHONE (310) █████████
FACSIMLE (310)█████████
E-MAIL ████████@aol.com

January 13, 2010

J. Morgan Dumont, III
9663 Santa Monica Blvd.
Box 274
Beverly Hills, CA 90210-4303

Re: <u>Inquiry Regarding Legal Representation</u>

Dear Mr. Dumont:

Today, I received your letter dated January 3, 2010, in which you requested legal assistance in conjunction with preparation of an anticipated family trust. Before I can provide you with my preliminary thoughts regarding the outlined objectives intended through the trust, and with an analysis of the pertinent issues, I ask that you contact me directly in order to schedule an in-person meeting with you. The description of your circumstances requires additional, extensive factual information before I am able to render an opinion thereon. Accordingly, it is essential that I obtain this information from you before I am able to offer legal assistance to you.

Please telephone me at your earliest convenience in order to arrange for a meeting in my office. I look forward to your next contact.

Very truly yours,

Interview Required
Drop In !!

████████████████

MICHAEL DAVID PRICE

J. MORGAN DUMONT, III

9663 SANTA MONICA BLVD., BOX 274
BEVERLY HILLS, CALIFORNIA 90210-4303

January 26, 2010

Michael David Price, Esq.
██████████████████
Suite ████
Los Angeles, California 90025

CONFIDENTIAL

Dear Mr. Price:

Thank you for your responsive letter of January 13, 2010. I appreciate your suggestion that I meet personally with you to discuss the trust in detail. Although I understand that Phineas is a minor and that his consent to the formation of this trust is not necessary, he would nevertheless like to attend, too.

We are available during the month of February to meet with you since, as you can imagine, the carnival season won't be starting for a couple of months. Unless I hear from you to the contrary, Phineas and I will be at your office at 10:00 a.m., on Thursday, February 10, 2010. I hope that date is convenient for you.

As I'm sure you can appreciate, it is important for revenue purposes to keep Phineas out of the public eye so as to ensure that the only way to catch a glimpse of him is to pay the price of admission at one of our shows. To that end, it is important that no photographs of Phineas be taken as they would no doubt be promptly sold to supermarket tabloids. Please advise your staff and other tenants, if any, at your office building. If you can't ensure compliance with this request, please advise. Although Phineas has a hood for outdoor activities, he doesn't like wearing it unless it is really necessary.

Also, does your office have a side or back entrance that is wheelchair accessible? This would help us to avoid gawking crowds. Thanks.

Very truly yours,

J. Morgan Dumont
J. Morgan Dumont

LAW OFFICES OF

MICHAEL DAVID PRICE

████████ BOULEVARD
SUITE ████
LOS ANGELES, CALIFORNIA 90025
TELEPHONE (310)████████
FACSIMLE (310)████████
E-MAIL ██████@aol.com

February 8, 2010

J. Morgan Dumont, III
9663 Santa Monica Blvd.
Box 274
Beverly Hills, CA 90210-4303

Dear Mr. Dumont:

Unfortunately, I am unavailable for an appointment on February 10, 2010. I am available however, on Friday, February 11, 2010 at 10:00 a.m. to meet with Phineas and you. Please contact my office in order to confirm your appointment.

Thank you again for your interest in my firm.

Very truly yours,

MICHAEL DAVID PRICE

J. MORGAN DUMONT, III

POST OFFICE BOX 192
MECHANICSVILLE, PENNSYLVANIA 18934-0192

February 10, 2010

PERSONAL DELIVERY
Michael David Price, Esq.
██████████████████████
Suite ██████
Los Angeles, California 90025

CONFIDENTIAL

Dear Mr. Price:

Thank you for your responsive letter. As you know, Phineas would like to attend, too, even though, as a minor, his presence is not really necessary. As suggested, Phineas and I will be at your office tomorrow, February 11, 2010, at 10:00 A.M. I'll bring all the necessary paperwork concerning Phineas' income and expenses.

As you can imagine, Phineas has some special needs which I hope you can accommodate at our meeting. Although he doesn't mind gawkers during carnival performances, he is very sensitive in other contexts. Specifically, he gets very upset when people stare at his eye. If he senses that your eyes remain too long on the middle of his forehead, he might throw a tantrum and start banging his sirenomeulus against a chair or table. So, please, try not to look at his eye. Thank you.

Very truly yours,

J. Morgan Dumont

J. Morgan Dumont

NO REPLY!

HANSON D. HARREVELD, P.A.
Attorney at Law

407-████
Fax 407-████
e-mail: ██████@aol.com

███████ Loop
Suite ████
Alamonte Springs, Florida 32701

March 1, 2010

J. Morgan Dumont, III
9663 Santa Monica Blvd.
Box 274
Beverly Hills, CA 90210-4303

RE: <u>CREATION OF TRUST FOR THE BENEFIT OF PHINEAS DUMONT</u>

Dear Mr. Dumont, III

I am in receipt of your letter dated February 10, 2010. I am more than willing to meet with you and work with you to create a trust even if you decide to serve as trustee yourself. I look forward to the opportunity to work with you on this project.

It appears from your letter that you would prefer to maintain control over the trust assets and thus serve as trustee yourself. Please remember that the trustee has a "fiduciary duty" and "duty of undivided loyalty" to the beneficiaries of the trust. The trustee is required to exercise great prudence in managing the trust, and to ensure that the trust assets are invested in such a way as to maximize income and gain.

With regard to the questions raised and the information that you provided to me in your letter, I can offer you the following information. As Phineas would be the beneficiary of this trust, you will have a fiduciary duty to act at all times in his best interest. The denial of trust benefits to Phineas, to motivate him to "honor his obligations to his parents", is problematic. Withholding basic needs such as food, clothing and shelter from Phineas for such purposes would clearly pose additional problems. Using your position as trustee to serve your own interests (e.g., requiring Phineas to perform) would also be problematic. Trustees may not act in any capacity which might be viewed as "self-dealing" or "self-serving". As trustee, you will have a duty of "undivided loyalty" to Phineas. Furthermore, as Phineas is a minor, he can "void" any contract (other than a contract for "necessities") he enters into before he reaches eighteen years of age. Phineas' ability to void contracts could countermand your ability to enforce employment contracts with Phineas. In any event, such adversarial positions between you and Phineas would create a conflict of interest. These matters cannot be adequately addressed in this letter, but I am willing to meet with you personally to allow me the opportunity to answer your questions more fully, and to address your concerns and the issues you have raised.

I look forward to working with you. I would suggest that we meet at this point. Please call me so you and I can schedule a meeting. I am confident that we can construct a trust within lawful limits in such a way as to provide you with the protections you seek while at the same time adequately providing for Phineas' needs.

Please do not hesitate to contact me if you have any questions. I look forward to hearing from you very soon.

With warm personal regards, I am

Very truly yours,

HANSON D. HAAREVELD, P.C.

HANSON D. HAAREVELD, ESQUIRE

Great!!
Hire this lawyer!!

J. MORGAN DUMONT, III

6901 W. OKEECHOBEE BLVD., D-5, BOX 161
WEST PALM BEACH, FLORIDA 33411

March 5, 2010

Hanson D. Haareveld, Esq.

████████████████████

Suite ██████
Altamonte Springs, Florida 32701

CONFIDENTIAL

Dear Mr. Haareveld:

It took a while, but it finally occurred to me why you are so reluctant to have me act as Phineas's trustee. It's clear that you see a fortune in fees for yourself—and maybe a little invasion of the corpus now and again for your personal benefit—if I permitted you to become the trustee instead. I asked you to help me get Phineas sufficiently intimidated so that he will honor his commitment to his family and thereby avoid countless lawsuits that will be brought against me if that little freak continues to strike. Instead of help, you gave me a lot of mumbo jumbo about "fiduciary duties" and the like, none of which helps me one jot.

If you're willing to help me secure financial freedom for my wife and myself, great. In that case, you're our man for the job, and we will compensate you generously. However, if you want to get rich usurping my position as Phineas' manager by maneuvering yourself into the position of his trustee, forget it. In that event, I suggest that you find your own Cyclops merman. Good luck.

You closed your last letter with these words: "I am confident that we can construct a trust within lawful limits in such a way as to provide you with the protections you seek while at the same time adequately providing for Phineas' needs". If you want my business, you'd better concentrate on how you plan to protect me. I've already been saddled with raising a freak, and I want my take assured. Unlike me, Phineas doesn't require much in the way of food or clothing, and there's certainly no reason why he should be educated. People don't throw money at my feet every day, but Phineas can earn a fortune by rolling out of bed, provided that someone is there to gawk at him while he does it. I'm the one that needs help!

I look forward to your prompt reply outlining your scheme to achieve my objectives.

Very truly yours,

J. Morgan Dumont

JMD/km

CHAPTER 9

Mr. Dumont and the Seed of Life

J. MORGAN DUMONT, III

9663 SANTA MONICA BLVD., BOX 274
BEVERLY HILLS, CALIFORNIA 90210-4303

January 15, 2010

Arthur T. Halloway, Esq.

████████████████████████

████████████

Los Angeles, California 90067

CONFIDENTIAL

Dear Mr. Halloway:

I'm in terrible trouble, and a mutual acquaintance has urged me to contact you. I realize that sophisticated litigation is expensive, and I am prepared to pay a non-refundable flat fee of $200,000 to the lawyer who I select. (I don't like paying professionals by the hour because it encourages inefficiency and waste.) Nevertheless, I realize that sophisticated litigation often costs more than $200,000, but I thought that you might be tempted to take my case if I paid a flat fee up front.

In order for you to understand the seriousness of this dispute and how painful it is to me personally, you need some background information. I love babies. I always have. There is nothing more awe inspiring than holding a newborn in your arms. Each is a miracle from God.

To parents like me, everything associated with their children is special, from the conception event, to the confirmation of pregnancy, to the first quickening in the womb, and, of course, to the birthing process. For many, bearing one's own child has no substitute. For them, failure to have a child of their own blood creates an open wound that even the passage of decades cannot heal.

As a result, ever since I was a young man (I am now 62 years old), I've wanted to devote my life to helping hopeful couples to have their own children. Accordingly, it has always been my dream to own and operate a fertility clinic in order to help disappointed partners to experience the ineffable joy of birth.

My grandfather and father were in the oil business, and I am independently wealthy. Because I did not want to attend medical school, it was necessary for me to bankroll a physician who, like me, wanted to open a fertility clinic. I found such a doctor. He was the perfect business partner. He had the medical degree but no money to invest in a clinic; I had abundant wealth but no license. I became the doctor's ghost partner. Of course, he conducted the medical procedures, but I ran the clinic. In this way, I have been able to participate in the joy of helping young people to have offspring. For 23 years, we have had a thriving practice, and I have enjoyed a fulfilled life.

Now our clinic is wholly dedicated to the process of in vitro fertilization. As wonderful as that process is, it has one serious drawback. It robs parents of the sexual intimacy that is a part of normal procreation. This is because the father is asked to retire to a private booth where he is expected to produce semen for the procedure. His sperm is delivered to the mother's receptive uterus during a sterile surgical procedure. Unfortunately, from the mother's perspective, in vitro fertilization denies her the experience of participating in her husband's contribution--the bringing forth of the seed of life.

The absence of love making is, of course, a serious drawback to in vitro fertilization. At the risk of appearing indiscrete, you should know that it is my personal belief that God gave men and women the ability to experience the ecstasy of orgasm in order to make the conception event memorable. Many mothers have privately lamented that they could not, like natural conception mothers, reminisce about the twinkle in their husband's eye, the caress of his hand or the smile on his face at the moment of sexual bliss. This defect in the process has always bothered me, and I resolved to do something about it.

My idea was as follows. Recall that hopeful husbands are asked to bring forth their seed in a private booth. In order to capture the moment of ecstasy in bringing forth the seed of life, I hid a camera in the booth directly above the father's chair. I never, ever looked at the film. If the mother never bore a child from her husband's seed, we simply threw the video out. However, if a child was eventually delivered, we gave our complementary Bringing Forth The Seed Of Life video to the happy parents on the child's first birthday. Again, in order to assure privacy, the members of my clinic have never viewed any of these videos.

Three months ago, we sent out our first batch of Bringing Forth the Seed of Life videos to our successful clients. However, last week, we received two angry telephone calls from the fathers about our videos. Apparently, their wives had opened the package and viewed the video DVDs in their absence. Because we had never watched the videos, we did not know that one of the husbands used a visual aid in bringing forth his seed-—Jugs Magazine. The other angry husband had facilitated fantacization by holding up a nude picture of his secretary.

Both these men say their wives are considering divorce, and both have threatened me with a lawsuit. In fact, one lawyer called the clinic and asked for the name of the clinic's "registered agent". That sounds bad to me.

I am interviewing one other lawyer, and I am asking both of you to give me your written preliminary thoughts as to what litigation strategy you would employ as well as your brief analysis of the issues. I will review and compare your replies in determining which lawyer should be retained. Kindly correspond with me promptly.

Very truly yours,

J. Morgan Dumont

J. Morgan Dumont, III

JMD/km

LAW OFFICES
ARTHUR T. HALLOWAY
SUITE ▇▇
1▇▇▇▇▇▇▇▇▇▇▇▇6
LOS ANGELES, CALIFORNIA 90067
(310) ▇▇▇▇▇
FAX (310) 5▇▇▇▇▇2

January 25, 2010

J. Morgan Dumont, III
9663 Santa Monica Blvd.
Box 274
Beverly Hills, CA 90210-4303

CONFIDENTIAL

RE: Bringing Forth The Seed Of Life

Dear Mr. Dumont:

I empathize with your situation and I believe that you're not the kind of man who would have gotten himself into this situation. I believe you do good for people and your life is evidence of this.

In response to your letter, I have the following preliminary ideas.

1. A Trial by Jury

I would request a trial by jury. I would request a jury trial because I believe you. I also believe that if you're in front of a jury of your peers, they will, also, believe you.

The benefit of jury trial would be that it would be more about justice and less about the LAW. To my way of thinking, this trial involves equitable considerations of what is fair and just, and it is far less about the law.

The issue (as I see it and would want the jury to see it) is this, ''whether it is fair and just to punish a good man, a man who served his community his whole life and a man who has meant no harm in his actions and only good". If you get the jury to feel this is the issue, then you may stand a chance of getting a favorable result.

2. Legal Defenses: (Consent and Privilege)

If an invasion of a person's right of privacy claim is filed or any other similar type of claim is made against you, you have two basic defenses:

Consent

You can argue that by consenting to invitro fertilization with your company, the husband and wife consented to your video recording (as one who goes to a department store and uses a dressing room to try on clothes consents to video camera). Furthermore, a right of privacy implies that you or your employees actually saw the video. You had never watched these videos nor did any of your employees, so there's no invasion of right of privacy.

Privilege

For the privilege situation, I would argue you had a medical privilege to make such taping because it was in the furtherance of science and I would use case law to back it up. More research needs to be done on this defense.)

3. Expert Testimony

Finally, I would support my arguments with expert testimony. In particular, I would use experts to prove your statement that, in fact, in vitro childbirth does leave women in want of more memorable experiences from the child conception moment as well.

If this letter bears any interest to you, please telephone my office for an appointment.

Very truly yours,

Arthur T. Halloway

Great !! Hire this lawyer !!

J. MORGAN DUMONT, III

9663 SANTA MONICA BLVD., BOX 274
BEVERLY HILLS, CALIFORNIA 90210-4303

February 11, 2010

Arthur T. Halloway, Esq.

Los Angeles, California 90067

CONFIDENTIAL

Dear Mr. Halloway:

Thank you for your well-considered reply letter of January 25, 2010. It has given me a lot to think about. When I first received the litigation threats from the two fathers, I was, frankly, cowed and inwardly concluded that I was somehow to blame for their problem. Since then, my thinking about this has turned 180 degrees. Now I'm angry, and I want to take the offensive.

In speaking with my partner (the physician), I learned some interesting facts about these two men. Naturally, when infertility is a problem, the reproductive organs of both spouses must be thoroughly checked out. My partner examined these men, and he has told me that they were both memorable because of their abnormally small genitalia. In fact, the husband who facilitated masturbation with Jugs Magazine was so tiny where it counts that my partner remarked that his so-called "manhood" looked more like a nipple than a penis. As to the other frivolous litigant, my partner remembered that his "member" (even when fully aroused) was about half the length of a normal peanut shell (not the jumbo kind that you sometimes see at specialty shops).

It occurred to me that if these (so-called) men are going to sue me, they'll have to play the dvd in front of a jury in open court. Maybe we should send a letter to their lawyers explaining that we are willing to offer only a small settlement because we do not believe that their clients will actually proceed with the action. In that letter, we could remind them that the actual size of their clients' manhood will be exposed in open court and, as a result, their clients will become the objects of social ridicule.

What do you think? Also, please advise as to when you are free to consult with me in person.

Very truly yours,

J. Morgan Dumont

J. Morgan Dumont

LAW OFFICES

ARTHUR T. HALLOWAY

SUITE ██

1█████████████████████

LOS ANGELES, CALIFORNIA 90067

(310) █████████

FAX (310) ███████████

CONFIDENTIAL

February 17, 2010

J. Morgan Dumont, III
9663 Santa Monica Blvd.
Box 274
Beverly Hills, CA 90210-4303

Dear Mr. Dumont:

Thank you for your letter of February 11, 2010. Although I understand your anger and frustration, I don't think it would be wise to force a quick settlement by threatening to humiliate the husbands of your former clients by airing the dvd in open court. Neither you nor I should conduct ourselves in any manner that even hints of blackmail.

Nevertheless, your point is well taken that proceeding with the lawsuit against you will necessarily cause the dvd's to be played publicly, thereby exposing the plaintiffs' physical shortcomings. Their lawyers certainly know that the dvd's are critical evidence, and they will undoubtedly inform their clients that they will be seen by all who attend the trial, including the press. In other words, there is no need to specifically describe to my adversaries the nature of their clients' prospective humiliation if they insist upon obtaining a judgment against you since this will eventually occur to their clients without our intervention. If the public exposure of their unfortunate sexual endowments will deter them from proceeding to trial, it should be sufficient for me simply to identify the dvd's as evidence that we intend to use in your defense as part of the normal disclosure process required by the Court.

Please call for an appointment so that we can discuss these matters in person.

Very truly yours,

Arthur T. Halloway

Redner and Rouche, L.L.P.

ATTORNEYS AT LAW

█████████ CIRCLE
█████████ BOULEVARD
HOLLYWOOD, FL 33021-6751

MORTIMORE S. REDNER
GEORGE M. ROUCHE

(954) █████ BROWARD
(954) █████ FAX
(305) 3████ DADE
e-mail: █████████.com
█████████.net

January 11, 2010

J. Morgan Dumont, III
6901 W. Okeechobee Blvd.,
Box 161
West Palm Beach, FL 33411

Re: Letter dated January 5, 2010

Dear Mr. Morgan:

Thank you for your inquiry letter dated January 5, 2010. I am "of counsel" to Redner & Rouche, LLP. This firm (senior partner) has represented ████████ Hospital in Miami Beach for the past 20 years. I thought you might find that information useful and wanted you to know that I have reviewed the content of your letter with him to best address the issues and communicate with you.

We are convinced of the sincerity of your actions, but are also concerned about the legal implications of them at the same time. Certainly, if there were any secretive intent, ill will or closet pornographic intent to your actions, you would not have delivered these DVDs to the parents. Nevertheless, the video recording of persons in private situations carries legal implications. Interestingly, some states even have NO PROHIBITION against this act so long as sound is not recorded. Your letter did not mention whether or not this occurred.

You should know that we are NOT criminal defense attorneys and would need to refer you to others if you are pursued criminally. If you would like to come visit us, please telephone—we will be happy to meet you.

Very truly yours,

Law Offices of Redner & Rouche, LLP

By: Charles N. Olsen, Esq.

J. MORGAN DUMONT, III

6901 W. OKEECHOBEE BLVD., D-5, BOX 161
WEST PALM BEACH, FLORIDA 33411

January 19, 2010

Charles L. Olsen, Esq,
Redner & Rouche, LLP
████████████
Hollywood, FL. 33201████

CONFIDENTIAL

Dear Mr. Olsen:

Thank you for your reply correspondence of January 11, 2010. Preliminarily, you should know that my name is "Mr. Dumont," not "Mr. Morgan." Please address me as such.

I was really troubled by one aspect of your letter. You say that there are legal (and possible criminal) implications with respect to video recording people in "private situations". I think you must have misunderstood my initial letter to you. The men who are threatening to sue me were video recorded in <u>MY</u> place of business, not behind bedroom doors at their homes. Are you telling me that if I visited <u>YOUR</u> house and started masturbating in <u>YOUR</u> family room that you could be charged with a crime if you video recorded me whacking off in front of you? Where's the justice in that? Please advise.

Very truly yours,

J. Morgan Dumont

J. Morgan Dumont

Redner and Rouche, L.L.P.

ATTORNEYS AT LAW

████████ CIRCLE
████████ BOULEVARD
HOLLYWOOD, FL 33021-6751

MORTIMORE S. REDNER
GEORGE M. ROUCHE

(954) 8███████0 BROWARD
(954) 8███████8 FAX
(305) 3███████5 DADE
e-mail: ████████.com
████████.net

January 28, 2010

J. Morgan Dumont, III
6901 W. Okeechobee Blvd.,
Box 161
West Palm Beach, FL 33411

<u>Your letter of January 19</u>

Dear Mr. Dumont:

I understand your dismay concerning the state of the law with respect to the right to privacy. I also understand why you believe that it would be absurdly ironic for you to be liable since the activities involved occurred in your own place of business. However, I cannot adequately explain the law and the reasoning behind it in a short written reply. For now, suffice it to say that serious privacy issues are at stake. I can best explain those issues to you in person. To that end, I invite you to telephone my office to schedule a consultation so that I can clarify the law for you. I look forward to hearing from you.

Very truly yours,

Law Offices of Redner & Rouche, LLP

By: Charles L. Olsen

Great!!
Hire this Lawyer!!

J. MORGAN DUMONT, III

6901 W. OKEECHOBEE BLVD., D-5, BOX 161
WEST PALM BEACH, FLORIDA 33411

February 5, 2010

Charles L. Olsen, Esq,
Redner & Rouche, LLP
████████████████
Hollywood, FL. 33201-████

CONFIDENTIAL

Dear Mr. Olsen:

I received your letter of January 28, 2010. I suppose that I'll just have to trust your judgment that privacy issues are at stake and I await your detailed explanation when we meet. To that end, I'll drop in your office around noon on February 12, 2010.

By the way, I thought that it would be a nice icebreaker if I brought my collection of Bringing Forth the Seed of Life DVDs when we meet and watch them together. If we can have some private time, we could, with the benefit of drawn curtains or pulled shades, use these DVDs as an aide in helping us get better acquainted — well, that is, MUCH better acquainted.

See you on the 12th for my interview with my DVDs with the hope that they will stimulate more than just legal strategies.

Very truly yours,

J. Morgan Dumont

J. Morgan Dumont, III.

NO REPLY!

CHAPTER 10

Mr. Dumont's Just Reward

J. MORGAN DUMONT, III

POST OFFICE BOX 192
MECHANICSVILLE, PENNSYLVANIA 18934-0192

October 25, 2009

Samuel K. Dean, Esq.
██████████ Avenue
█████ Building
Suite █████
Narbeth, PA 19072

CONFIDENTIAL

Dear Mr. Dean:

I am in need of an attorney to help me enforce a written contract that has been breached by my lying neighbor who has cheated me out of $100,000 of compensation. I am independently wealthy, and I don't really need the money in order to live, but it is the principle of the matter I care about. I absolutely refuse to accept passively anyone's intentional deception, and I am willing to pay the attorney whom I select a substantial non-refundable flat fee of $50,000.00 to vindicate my rights in court. (I don't like paying attorneys by the hour because it encourages inefficiency and waste.) Again, I don't care (really) if I recover just one dollar of damages so long as my cheating neighbor is brought to task in a court of law.

By way of background, you should know that my next-door neighbor, April Muller, has been a thorn in my side for the last seven years. It is not just one thing about her that angers me, but rather, it is the accumulation of countless nuisances that together make her proximity to me intolerable. For example, she never mows her lawn, and her fifteen acre lot resembles a neglected hay field. Two years ago, a large tree blew over on her lawn near my prized sculpture garden, leaving branches and twigs strewn everywhere, and that mess has remained there to this day. The paint on her house is peeling off, and a once lovely home has now taken on the appearance of a depression era Midwest farmhouse. Muller has done nothing to remedy the situation notwithstanding my repeated demands that she hire painters.

She has neglected to maintain her residence in other ways, and it is now in such disrepair that it is starting to look abandoned. For example, for the last two years, she has done nothing to replace two cracked windowpanes in the front of her house. One window shutter on the second floor has become partially detached and now dangles upside down. Even the guesthouse on her estate looks more cared for that the main residence. In truth, her home looks like a hovel belonging to some inner city low life. It's embarrassing to live next to her. I feel as if I am dwelling at the edge of a ghetto.

Muller has plenty of money, and she can easily afford to care for her property. In fact, she is wealthy as a result of a large litigation settlement with respect to a car accident with a gasoline tanker that left her parents dead and her permanently blind. Seven years ago, when she reached 21 years of age, the bank that functioned as her court-appointed trustee distributed the entire litigation settlement from trust to her directly. Unfortunately, she used this distribution to purchase the home next to mine. A friend of mine told me that Muller's settlement with the oil company was enormous, so there's no excuse for neglecting her responsibilities as my neighbor. As you can tell, I am furious that I have been forced to endure her presence on my street. I've suffered enough.

My need for legal counsel arose one week ago when I was pulling out of my driveway. At that time, I ran over a dog that had been allowed to roam loose. It didn't die right away, but rather, it dragged itself off my driveway, so I it wasn't put out by having to move its carcass.

Two days after hitting that mutt, I played a round of golf at my country club, and when I returned to my car, someone had stuffed a handwritten flyer under the windshield wiper of my Rolls. I couldn't believe my luck. April Muller was offering a $100,000.00 reward for the return of her Seeing Eye dog. I will quote that flyer verbatim:

> Desperate to find valuable guide dog. The dog, named Oscar, is a chocolate colored Labrador retriever who is only 14 months old. When it ran away, it was wearing a leather harness typically worn for dogs trained for the blind. Oscar's owner offers $100,000.00 for information leading to his whereabouts.

The flyer provided April Muller's name, address and telephone number.

I instantly remembered that the mutt that I ran over a few days before had been wearing such a leather contraption, and I now surmised that this lost dog was the same one that I had accidentally dispatched.

Anxious to claim the $100,000.00 reward, I immediately returned to my driveway and followed the stained trail from where I had run over the dog. I found the mutt's bloody carcass on my property a few hundred feet away from my driveway. I then dragged it to Muller's front door, and when she answered, I presented her with her own flyer in which she had promised the reward. I explained to her that I had accidentally killed her animal after it had trespassed on my property. I then took her hand and planted it on its stiffened remains.

Muller became hysterical, and she immediately reneged on her promise to pay the $100,000.00. She acted as if she had never offered any reward at all, lamely arguing that she had conditioned her obligation to pay it upon the mutt's safe return. Of course, the flyer stated only that the reward was being offered for "information leading to [the dog's] whereabouts". I did a lot more that just give Muller "information" about the animal's "whereabouts". I delivered it directly to her doorstep.

I'm sick and tired of Muller's irresponsibility and unconscionable conduct. For once, I'm going to see to it that she lives up to her obligations. I am interviewing one other attorney, and I want to select an advocate who will insist that a person's word is her bond and should be held accountable. Can you help me obtain justice? Do you see any special problems with my case? Please advise.

I look forward to hearing from you, and I hope that we can enter a mutually profitable relationship. <u>By the way, if you see any way in which I can use the coercive power of the court to force Muller to maintain her property, I would be VERY interested in getting your thoughts on that issue.</u> I would gladly advance an additional non-refundable flat fee in an amount acceptable to you for prosecuting such a lawsuit. Thank you.

Very truly yours,

J. Morgan Dumont, III

JMD/km

P.S. That animal dinged up the front fender of my Rolls Royce when I ran over it, and I need to know whether I can get damages from Muller for negligently allowing the beast to trespass on my property. I don't think that I should be burdened with the repair costs. Please advise.

The Law Offices of

SAMUEL K. DEAN

A PROFESSIONAL ASSOCIATION

Samuel K. Dean, Esquire
Sarah M. Dean, Esquire
Thomas A. Parker, Esquire
_____

Hardin W. Jameson, Paralegal

████████ Building
████████ Avenue, Suite ██
Narbeth, PA 19072

Telephone: (407) ████████
Facsimile: (407) ████████
E-Mail: ████████o.com

October 30, 2009

J. Morgan Dumont, III
P.O. Box 192
Mechanicsville, PA 19834-0912

Re: Your dispute with April Muller

Dear Mr. Dumont:

Thank you for your letter of October 25, 2009, which I found very interesting. Kindly identify our mutual friend so that I can than him or her for this referral.

I would be happy to represent you in the various matters raised in your letter. Some will be more difficult to achieve than others. Let me address your issues in order of ascending difficulty.

Even disabled people have to comply with municipal ordinances with respect to the upkeep of property. Increasingly, municipalities have extended the duty to maintain property beyond the obligation to comply with safety codes and are enforcing some types of aesthetic requirements. However, without knowing the municipality in which Ms. Muller resides, I cannot examine the relevant municipal ordinances as to what violations, if any, exist at her residence. Assuming the property does not comply with applicable municipal ordinances and codes, obtaining relief should be fairly straightforward.

Obtaining a judgment for damages caused to your Rolls Royce will be a little tougher. If the dog was roaming loose on your property, that constitutes negligence on Ms. Muller's part, and the damage caused to your car when it ran into your path on your own driveway should be charged to Ms. Muller. I note two potential issues in this respect, however. First, you could open yourself up to an accusation by way of an affirmative defense that you were contributorily negligent (speeding, for example) and that Muller is therefore only partly responsible for the damages suffered to your Rolls Royce. More facts would have to be developed in order to evaluate your exposure to such a defense. Second, sympathy for Ms. Muller as a result of her blindness, disfigurement and loss of her companion might well result in jury nullification, i.e., the jury's decision to hold in favor of Ms. Muller even though the jurors know that the law requires a different result.

Obtaining a judgment for Ms. Muller's breach of her promise to pay a $100,000 reward that you describe would be the most problematic of tasks. First, the risk of jury nullification as a result of jurors' sympathy toward Ms. Muller would, in my opinion, be very high. Most jurors would probably feel great compassion for this unfortunate defendant who lost not only her pet, but also a trusted companion. The fact that you appear to be wealthy will not help your cause, either, since some jurors might conclude that your quest for a monetary reward (that you don't really need to make ends meet) will force Ms. Muller to relive another life tragedy on top of her scarred body and loss of sight.

Second, you are correct that the strict, literal interpretation of the reward mandates that Ms. Muller pay you $100,000 since you solved the problem about the dog's "whereabouts". However, a court might hold that the only reasonable interpretation of the reward offer is to achieve the dog's safe return. Muller would certainly argue that she was not offering an "Old West," "WANTED-DEAD-OR-ALIVE" reward. She'll contend that the reward's purpose was not to take the dog out of circulation as it is with a wanted criminal, but rather, it was designed to achieve the dog's safe return.

Third, I am concerned that the manner in which you attempted to collect your reward might be interpreted by some overly sensitive jurors as being callous and emotionally injurious to Ms. Muller. For example, your forcing her hand on the stiffened remains of her deceased companion might offend some jurors, and if you said anything to her that would shock the conscience of a reasonable person while you did this, you might well open yourself up to a counterclaim for intentional or negligent infliction of emotional distress. I would have to interview you further in order to ascertain the full extent of your potential liability, if any, to such a potential counterclaim.

In any event, I will have to interview you further in order to flesh out the facts relevant to your claim as well as to any possible affirmative defenses or counterclaims that could be asserted against you. That having been said, if you are willing to proceed after being fully apprised of the risks, I would be happy to represent you on the terms stated in your letter. Please telephone my office for an appointment. I look forward to meeting you.

Sincerely,

Samuel K. Dean

Great!! Hire this lawyer!!

J. MORGAN DUMONT, III

POST OFFICE BOX 192
MECHANICSVILLE, PENNSYLVANIA 18934-0192

November 7, 2009

Samuel K. Dean, Esq.
████████ Avenue
████ Building
Suite ███
Narbeth, PA 19072

CONFIDENTIAL

Dear Mr. Dean:

Thank you for your dynamite letter of October 30. I definitely want to meet with you and eventually retain you. To hell with the litigation risks! I want that bitch, April Muller, to get exactly what she deserves, even if it subjects me to her frivolous claims.

Your letter got me to thinking about the damage to my Rolls and how the bitch might claim that I was contributorily negligent when her Seeing Eye dog, Oscar, ran under my automobile. I have been told by a forensic technician who works for the FBI that if a corpse from a pedestrian traffic accident has tread marks imbedded on his skin, you can calculate from the relative distortion of those tread marks how fast the vehicle was traveling at the time of impact. I can assure you that I was not traveling more than 20 miles an hour on my driveway, and after I got your letter, I thought of a way to prove it.

I had the caretaker of my property enter Muller's land and exhume Oscar's remains where she buried him. (The bitch is blind, so no one was the wiser). Just as my FBI contact had explained, Oscar's hind quarters (once shaved) show the presence of nearly distortion-free tread marks, proving that I was not traveling at a significant speed.

I intend to drop in your office on Tuesday, November 15, 2009, so that you can interview me and inspect the tread mark evidence. Accordingly, I suggest that you and your staff purchase respirators so that my interview will be as comfortable as possible.

On last complication: When shaving Oscar's hindquarters in order to view the tire marks, I noticed that he had been hit with some birdshot. Recall that when living, Oscar had repeatedly roamed onto my property, and I routinely tried to wing it with some birdshot in order to get that mutt moving off my land. It appears that my aim was pretty good the night when Oscar met his maker, though the gunshot injury itself wasn't fatal. I mention this only because I can envision some nonsense argument that it was my fault for running Oscar over because his injury prevented him from moving out of my path quickly enough. Please confirm that this "glitch" in the evidence does not pose any serious problems. Thank you, and I look forward to meeting with you.

Very truly yours,

J. Morgan Dumont, III

JMD/km

P.S. I will bring a cheap, disposable card table with me as well as some plastic sheeting so as to make sure that nothing in your office gets contaminated as a result of our inspection of Oscar's remains.

The Law Offices of

SAMUEL K. DEAN

A PROFESSIONAL ASSOCIATION

Samuel K. Dean, Esquire
Sarah M. Dean, Esquire
Thomas A. Parker, Esquire

Hardin W. Jameson, Paralegal

 Building
Avenue, Suite
Narbeth, PA 19072

Telephone: (407)
Facsimile: (407)
E-Mail: ⬛.com

ATTORNEY-CLIENT PRIVILEGED

November 10, 2009
J. Morgan Dumont, III
P.O. Box 192
Mechanicsville, PA 19834-0912

> **Re: April Muller**

Dear Mr. Dumont:

I received with alarm your letter of November 7, 2009. Although I can understand the integrity of your motive for entering Ms. Muller's property, the exhumation of the guide dog's remains without permission constitutes trespass for which you may be held criminally and civilly liable. Therefore, I would not be able to use any evidence taken from the dog's exhumed body without exposing you to serious liability. Accordingly, there is no reason for you to arrive at my office with the dog's remains. I hope that this letter is received by you before your arrival since you have not provided me with your telephone number. The bottom line is that I cannot have the animal's carcass in my office for any reason. Please telephone me upon your receipt of this letter.

Sincerely,

Samuel K. Dean

J. MORGAN DUMONT, III

POST OFFICE BOX 192
MECHANICSVILLE, PENNSYLVANIA 18934-0192

November 14, 2009

Samuel K. Dean, Esq.
▮▮▮▮▮▮▮Avenue
▮▮▮▮▮▮▮Building

CONFIDENTIAL

Suite ▮▮▮▮
Narbeth, PA 19072

Dear Mr. Dean:

I am in receipt of your mambie pambie letter of November 10. Tresspass/schmesspass. What do I care if I get fined in municipal court a few bucks for being on Muller's land without her permission? I doubt that they're going to lock me up and throw away the key just because I dug up a dead dog! I want that reward money, and this trespass business isn't going to stop me from getting what's mine. In other words, I take full responsibility for the risks of proceeding with the evidence of tire tracks on Oscar's hindquarters, and I will gladly release you from any liability for proceeding since you have fully advised me of the risks.

We were originally supposed to meet tomorrow, but your letter threw me for a loop, and will have to drop in your office soon in order to conduct the inspection of Oscar's carcass. Inspecting the carcass sooner than later has become imperative since Oscar's decay is advancing rapidly and he's starting to drip a bit. To that end, I will drop in your office on November 18, 2009, at 11:00 a.m. I'll provide the respirators for you and your staff as well as the other equipment needed to keep Oscar from dripping onto your carpet.

Very truly yours,

J. Morgan Dumont

J. Morgan Dumont, III

JMD/km

The Law Offices of

SAMUEL K. DEAN

A PROFESSIONAL ASSOCIATION

Samuel K. Dean, Esquire
Sarah M. Dean, Esquire
Thomas A. Parker, Esquire

Hardin W. Jameson, Paralegal

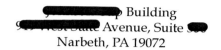 Building
Avenue, Suite
Narbeth, PA 19072

Telephone: (407)
Facsimile: (407)
E-Mail: o.com

ATTORNEY-CLIENT PRIVILEGED

November 16, 2009
PRIORITY MAIL

J. Morgan Dumont, III
P.O. Box 192
Mechanicsville, PA 19834-0912

Re: April Muller

Dear Mr. Dumont:

I have your letter of November 14, 2009. Please, under no circumstances, arrive at my office with the dog's decaying remains. My secretary has promised to resign if the inspection proceeds in our office on the 18th or on any other day. Finally, because of the hectic nature of my schedule, you will need to telephone me first in order to schedule an appointment by yourself and without the dog. You cooperation in this regard would be appreciated.

Sincerely,

Samuel K. Dean

CHAPTER 11

Mr. Dumont
– The Merkin Mavin

J. MORGAN DUMONT, III

9812 FALLS ROAD, SUITE 114, BOX 300
POTOMAC, MARYLAND 20854

January 5, 2010

Ester Z. Goldberg, Esq.
Ester Z. Goldberg and Associates
████████████████████
Suite ████
Bethesda, MD 20814

CONFIDENTIAL

Dear Ms. Goldberg:

I need the help of a trial lawyer with respect to a lawsuit. I realize that legal assistance for sophisticated litigation is not cheap, and I am prepared to pay an up front, non-refundable flat fee of $200,000 to the lawyer who I select. I don't like paying lawyers by the hour because it encourages inefficiency and waste. Although I realize that sophisticated litigation often costs more than $200,000, I thought that you might nevertheless be tempted to take my case if I paid a flat fee up front.

In order for you to assist me, I need to give you some background. When I was a boy, I knew that I would inherit a fortune from my father who was in the uranium mining industry. As a result, I was not a motivated student and I spent more time climbing the timbered hills of New Mexico than I did in the classroom. I never obtained my high school degree.

Both my parents had passed away by my nineteenth birthday. I was a rich kid without direction. From my teens through my early fifties, I played continuously. My life had no purpose, no meaning. Then things changed quickly. I won't bore you with the details, but when I was 54, I contracted a disease and nearly died. I was faced with the prospect of dying without having accomplished anything worthwhile. During the months following my recovery, I tried to find some way to help others in order to give my life meaning.

The prospect of a career inside a hospital immediately attracted me. More than anything else, I wanted to become a physician. However, I knew that my lack of education killed that possibility. I would have gladly become a male nurse if I had gone to college. I was willing to do anything that would help people. Accordingly,

I became an orderly on the cancer floor of my local hospital, emptying bed pans, changing linen and cleaning bathrooms. While working there, I noticed that the chemotherapy that was administered to patients caused them to lose their hair. As you can imagine, baldness is particularly devastating to girls and women, and after seeing one particularly pretty 16 year old girl fall to pieces after looking in the mirror, I decided to do something about it. I traveled to a local wig manufacturer and purchased several hundred of his best wigs in all colors, styles and lengths for the patients. I was determined not to bring back synthetic "mops" for their heads. Instead, I bought the very best wigs made out of 100% natural hair. At that time (13 years ago), each wig cost over $500. However, since I am rich, I could easily afford them.

The wigs caused a sensation. I helped each patient pick them out. I styled each wig to please the individual and made sure that each fitted perfectly. Word spread among several hospitals in our State that I was an expert at wigs and hairpieces, and I quit my job in order to do the same charitable work in other hospitals. The secret to my success was quality. I had the money to purchase the very best natural wigs, and I made sure that each wig was made with luxuriant natural human hair. Finally, my life had meaning.

One day when I went to the wig factory, the owner told me that he was going out of business because competing wig manufacturers that used synthetic fibers were able to sell their products at prices that were dramatically lower than his. The prospect of disappointing those poor patients by losing my local supply of high-quality, all natural wigs really upset me. I know it was impulsive, but I immediately offered to buy his plant. Before I knew it, I was in the wig business full time, responsible for over 200 employees. Although I continued to donate wigs to local hospitals, I quickly realized that I had to run the plant like a business, not a charity, in order to pay salaries and benefits to my employees.

I kept my contacts in the medical community, and I continued to offer special services to hospitals. One day, an oncologist said in an offhanded way that it was unfortunate that I limited my production of wigs to just head coverings. I instinctively laughed, but he assured me that he was serious. He explained to me that the loss of pubic hair was embarrassing in the bedroom and was especially disturbing for men. He explained that pubic baldness sometimes impairs intimacy and contributes to sexual dysfunction. He also explained to me that there were other ailments and diseases other than cancer that prevent the production of estrogen and androgen in females and males, respectively, and cause loss of pubic hair. Hormonal deficiencies that delay or prevent the onset of puberty (and concomitant growth of pubic hair) can cause humiliation for adolescents in the locker room. Infection of pubic louse (crabs) is best treated by medication applied to a bare pubic area. Obviously, this means shaving the pubic hair which creates the warm, moist bacterial-laden condition in which pubic louse thrive. The doctor told me that individuals undergoing therapy for crabs would probably prefer to wear a pubic wig (if they knew such wigs were available) so as not to tip off their partner that they were being treated for the eradication of a sexually transmitted parasite. The oncologist assured me that there was a real medical need for pubic wigs, and I told him that I would do my best to create these most personal of hairpieces for his patients.

I was astonished to learn that the concept of a pubic wig is not new. In fact, these hairpieces were commonly worn during the 18th Century, when wig wearing had reached the height of popularity. There is even a special name for a pubic wig—a "merkin." I researched old French texts on hairdressing in order to learn how merkins were made, and I soon manufactured my first prototype.

As my father used to say, the key to success is being in the right place at the right time. I had stumbled upon a new (yet ironically, old) product for which there was a wide-spread (though discrete) demand. Like the wigs we produce, our merkins are made of only top-quality human hair, not synthetics. Advertisements for my merkins were placed in every medical supply catalog throughout the world. Soon, my merkins were selling like hotcakes.

In last three years, my merkins became more popular as specialty fashion items than they were as medical prosthetics. "Fashion merkins", as I call them, are strictly a feminine product. There is a class of affluent, sexually active women who frequently change their hair color. After each dye job, they want the collars to match the cuffs, metaphorically speaking. The caustic chemicals and (possible) carcinogens in popular hair dyes make it impractical to apply them close to the female genitalia. Because our merkins are made with all-natural, human hair, they can be repeatedly died to match the tint of the wearer's head hair.

I'm proud to say that I am the only merkin manufacturer in existence, and anyone who wants a pubic wig must buy one from me. Lately, there has been a run on merkins. Within the last six months, production has fallen well behind demand. To make matters worse, the supply of natural hair for my merkins shriveled up. Let me explain.

As you know, pubic hair is universally kinky. Merkins cannot be manufactured by "perming" straight into kinky hair. It is imperative that hair used for a merkin must be naturally kinky. Harvesting pubic hair is, for health and modesty reasons, out of the question. Of course, the answer was to contract with several hundred Negroes for them to periodically shave the hair on their heads and sell it to me. This I did, and they entered into long-term requirement contracts for which they were paid handsomely. I did not, however, tell my Negro suppliers how their hair was being used, and they apparently assumed that it was being manufactured into traditional wigs. Last month, my Negro suppliers discovered that I was using their hair for pubic wigs, and they immediately went on strike. Within a week, I didn't have a single curlicue left with which to make a merkin.

I am now in desperate straits. We have tried in vain to create merkins from Caucasian hair, but, after a few wearings and poundings, they soon revert to their former texture and end up looking like little triangular horse manes. This is unacceptable.

A lawyer acquaintance told me that I will never get a court to order my Negro suppliers to shave their heads. He said that a purchaser of goods cannot compel performance of the contract (i.e., requiring them to deliver their head hair to me) because (to use his words), I am not "immediately" faced with "irreparable harm." But that's not true! My entire manufacturing business is about to go under and nearly two hundred jobs will be lost if I can't produce merkins fast. Wouldn't a court find such a harm to be irreparable? Isn't there some litigation strategy that can be employed to make sure that my Negro suppliers honor their contracts before it's too late?

I am interviewing one other lawyer, and I am asking both of you to give me your written preliminary analysis. I will review and compare your replies in determining which lawyer should be retained. Kindly correspond with me promptly.

Very truly yours,

J. Morgan Dumont

J. Morgan Dumont, III

LAW OFFICES
ESTER Z. GOLDBERG AND ASSOCIATES
A Professional Corporation

▓▓▓▓▓▓▓▓▓▓▓▓▓

SUITE 4▓▓▓▓

BETHESDA, MARYLAND 20814

(301) ▓▓▓▓▓▓

TELECOPIER: (301) ▓▓▓▓▓▓

January 26, 2010

J. Morgan Dumont, III
9812 Falls Road, Suite 114
Box 300
Potomac, MD 20854

Dear Mr. Dumont:

This is in response to your letter of January 5, 2010. Thank you for considering Ester Z. Goldberg and Associates to represent you in resolving the issue with your suppliers to compel performance of their contract.

It is the policy of this office to provide legal advice during an appointment with clients in this office. It is important that there be a face to face meeting between client and lawyer to insure that both the client and the lawyer are comfortable in dealing with one another. The office also does not provide legal opinions unless an attorney-client relationship is established. There is an hourly charge for the initial consultation. Please phone our office to schedule an appointment so that we can discuss this situation.

Sincerely,

Ester Z. Goldberg

EZD/aal

Interview Required
Drop In!!

J. MORGAN DUMONT, III

9812 FALLS ROAD, SUITE 114, BOX 300
POTOMAC, MARYLAND 20854

February 8, 2010

Ester Z. Goldberg, Esq.

Suite ████

Bethesda, Maryland 20814

CONFIDENTIAL

Dear Ms. Goldberg:

Thank you for your reply letter of January 26, 2010. On further reflection, your suggestion that I come in for a personal meeting is best. Unless it is inconvenient for you, I will drop in at your office sometime next week.

In order for you to fully appreciate my industry, I will bring a video DVD that my company provides to medical supply distributors who sell my merkins to pharmacies and hospitals. It is a high production value color video that will no doubt be helpful when explaining to a judge or jury how my business operates and the choices of medical and fashion merkins that are available to the public. It's a tastefully-done presentation and should go a long way in convincing a judge that my suppliers and their hair are being treated with dignity.

The video shows in detail how merkins are made. Our models also display the color varieties of our merkins and how they are applied and removed. It also shows how durable and hard-wearing they are. For example, we have filmed a runner on a treadmill as well as a female gymnast exercising on a balance beam while wearing one of my merkins.

Since you probably don't have a television and DVD player at your office, I'll bring them with me so that we can watch the video together. I'll also bring in a sample merkin or two for your inspection, which you can keep, if you so desire.

I look forward to meeting you.

Very truly yours,

J. Morgan Dumont

J. Morgan Dumont

LAW OFFICES

ESTER Z. GOLDBERG AND ASSOCIATES

A Professional Corporation

SUITE 4▮▮▮▮▮
BETHESDA, MARYLAND 20814

(301) ▮▮▮▮▮
TELECOPIER: (301)▮▮▮▮▮

February 15, 2010

J. Morgan Dumont, III
9812 Falls Road, Suite 114
Box 300
Potomac, MD 20854

Dear Mr. Dumont:

In response to your letter dated February 8, 2010. As I indicated in my previous letter, it is my policy to have an in person consultation with all new clients. I appreciate your offer to just drop by my office. However, because my schedule is extremely busy, it would be expeditious to call my assistant and schedule an appointment to avoid your arriving at a time when I am either with a client or out of the office.

Although I appreciate your offer to review a dvd promotional presentation of your product that you believe should be presented to a jury, it is premature to concentrate on what evidence should or should not be proffered. Instead, our initial consultation should focus on obtaining all the relevant facts, as well as making sure that there is no conflict of interest in my acting as your attorney. Also, I decline (with my thanks) your offer to give me a sample of your product, although you may bring one with you for me to inspect only.

Once again, please telephone my assistant in order for an appointment. Thank you.

Sincerely,

Ester Z. Goldberg

J. MORGAN DUMONT, III

**9812 FALLS ROAD, SUITE 114, BOX 300
POTOMAC, MARYLAND 20854**

February 23, 2010

Ester Z. Goldberg, Esq.
Ester Z. Goldberg and Associates
██████████████
Suite ████
Bethesda, MD 20814

CONFIDENTIAL

Dear Ms. Goldberg:

My predicament is now dire. Today, a camera crew from CBS's "60 Minutes" show arrived at my office to interview me about the "charges" that my merkin business exploits Negroes. I got befuddled in the glare of the camera lights and confused by the suddenness of the confrontation. I didn't know what to say except "no comment". When they pressured me for more information, I blurted out that I intended to use the judicial process to enforce my rights against my breaching Negro suppliers. In this regard, I told the show's producer that you were my attorney and that all questions regarding the merkin/Negro issue should be directed to you. I'm sure that these people will arrive at your office, so I wanted to give you the "heads up".

I realize that I jumped the gun when I told the "60 Minutes" television crew that you were definitely representing me, but I felt ambushed and I panicked. I am very sorry. Please forgive me. However, I guess the silver lining in this cloud is that it has accelerated my choice of legal representation. I know you will be an aggressive champion of my rights.

I look forward to your immediate reply.

Very truly yours,

J. Morgan Dumont

J. Morgan Dumont

JMD/km

LAW OFFICES
ESTER Z. GOLDBERG AND ASSOCIATES
A Professional Corporation

███████████████

SUITE 4████████
BETHESDA, MARYLAND 20814

(301) ████████
TELECOPIER: (301)████████

February 25, 2010

<u>Hand Delivered</u>
J. Morgan Dumont, III
9812 Falls Road, Suite 114
P. O. Box 300
Potomac, MD 20854

I was shocked by your letter of February 23. No attorney-client relationship between us exists. As you have recognized in your own letter, I have not agreed to represent you. Nor will I. Attorney/client relationships are based upon trust. Although I understand why you might have panicked, your misrepresentation to the producer of *60 Minutes* to the effect that I am your legal representative was indefensible. It has demonstrated to me that I will not be able to trust you. Therefore, I will not agree to be your lawyer.

I expect you to immediately telephone CBS and explain that I am not, and have never been, either your personal or company attorney. I urge you to do this immediately, since I don't want to be forced into disclosing to the 60 Minutes interviewer that you lied when you told CBS that I have agreed to represent you.

Sincerely,

Ester Z. Goldberg

Keith L. Mason
Attorney

Pauline Copeland
Legal Assistant

Law Office of
Keith L. Mason, Inc.
Attorney at Law
████████ Street, Antioch, California 04500

Telephone (925) ████
Facsimile (925) ████
E-mail: ████████e.com
www.keithmason.com

February 4, 2010

J. Morgan Dumont, III
9663 Santa Monica Blvd.
Box 274
Beverly Hills, CA 90210-4303

Dear Mr. Dumont:

I would be less than candid if I didn't tell you that your letter is the most bizarre unsolicited correspondence I have ever received. However, not to sound skeptical, I don't know anybody who would spend so much energy on a rouse. Therefore, I assume you are acting in good faith.

Frankly I don't think that the legal issue is all that sophisticated. However, without seeing the contract itself, it is impossible to give you specific legal advice. I am not sure that I agree with your lawyer friend regarding the possibility of obtaining injunctive relief from the hair suppliers. I would have to see the agreements to further opine.

However it would seem to me that you may not really need litigation. It would seem to be more expedient and cheaper to go elsewhere for your supplies. For instance, obtaining any other source within the States or outside the States. It occurs to me that those in third world countries might jump at the chance to shave their hair once every couple of months for American dollars. Then you would have the advantage of full control of the situation.

Please forward me copies of your agreement with this individual suppliers, and we will be able to give you specific advice.

Sincerely,

LAW OFFICES OF KEITH L. MASON

KEITH L. MASON
Attorney at Law

Great !!
Hire this Lawyer !!

KLM/km

J. MORGAN DUMONT, III

9663 SANTA MONICA BLVD., BOX 274
BEVERLY HILLS, CALIFORNIA 90210-4303

February 24, 2010

Keith L. Mason, Esq.
███████████████
██████ California 94509

CONFIDENTIAL

Dear Mr. Mason:

Thank you for your reply letter of February 4, 2010. I've decided to visit you for a consultation. Unless it is unacceptable to you, I'll be dropping by on March 8, 2010, at 11:00.

Unfortunately, your proposed solution about getting hair for my merkins from Third World donors won't work. There is an absurd moratorium in the United States on the importation of human body parts, which, believe it or not, has been deemed to encompass both fingernails and hair. I understand that we can thank our country's participation in the United Nations for this ridiculous result.

I need hair for my merkins desperately since I am now paying salaries out of my own pocket. Therefore, in addition to a legal action against my Negro suppliers, I would appreciate it if you could consider the following possible interim emergency solution. As you know, for both modesty and health reasons, the shearing of real pubic hair for my merkins has been out of the question. However, it recently occurred to me that I might be able to get real pubic hair without worrying about health or modesty issues. In this way, I can break the stranglehold that my Negro suppliers have on merkin production.

Let me explain. I have a friend who owns a large chain of funeral homes. He wants to help me out, and he's suggested that his staff could shear pubic hair from corpses for use in making merkins. Obviously, there would be no modesty problem since the donor would be dead, and the sterile setting of the mortician's lab would eliminate associated health problems, especially if the harvesting of hair occurs after the donor-corpse has been embalmed. My friend is confident that the procurement of pubic hair by shearing cadavers will work without anyone being the wiser.

Everyone knows that undertakers provide hair-cutting and beautician services, especially when the deceased is a female. Hair clippings from the dead are normally just thrown out. All I'm suggesting is this--when haircuts are ordered for the deceased in preparation for his or her viewing, the mortician do a whole-body job.

My undertaker friend says that, in his 35-year experience as an undertaker, no bereaved person has ever seen a naked corpse. He insists that, even if bereaved persons viewed a corpse whose pubic area were bald, the funeral home could tell them that the deceased's private parts were sheared in accordance with industry practice. What do you think? Please advise.

Very truly yours,

J. Morgan Dumont

J. Morgan Dumont

Keith L. Mason
Attorney

Pauline Copeland
Legal Assistant

Law Office of
Keith L. Mason, Inc.
Attorney at Law
██████████ Street, Antioch, California 04500

Telephone (925) ████
Facsimile (925) ████
E-mail: ███████.com
www.keithmason.com

March 2, 2010

J. Morgan Dumont, III
9663 Santa Monica Blvd.
Box 274
Beverly Hills, CA 90210-4303

Dear Mr. Dumont:

I am in receipt of your letter dated February 24, 2010. I must advise you that I will be out of the country on March 8, 2010 and will not be back to my office until March 14th.

You can contact my office at the telephone number indicated above, and make arrangements with my staff for a consultation after my return.

I look forward to meeting you.

Sincerely,

KEITH L. MASON
Attorney at Law

KLM/km

J. MORGAN DUMONT, III

9663 SANTA MONICA BLVD., BOX 274
BEVERLY HILLS, CALIFORNIA 90210-4303

March 4, 2010

Via Priority Mail

CONFIDENTIAL

Keith L. Mason, Esq.
███████████
██████ California 94509

Dear Mr. Mason:

I have sent this letter by priority mail, hoping that it will arrive before you leave the country on the 8th. I wish you had told me earlier that you were taking a vacation abroad. I have a private jet that is capable of transatlantic flight, and flying together to your destination would give us the perfect opportunity to discuss the resolution of my Negro supplier strike that is destroying my merkin business. Although this might seem too forward, maybe we can vacation together? I desperately need to get away from the stress caused by the striking Negroes, and a trip to Europe would be the perfect tonic. I hope you can cancel your travel arrangements so that you can go with me instead. I think you'll find my jet to be far more comfortable than any commercial liner. I will telephone your office for your reply.

By the way, when I read your letter of March 2, I was gratified not to see any objections to my plan to obtain real pubic hair from funeral home operators. I immediately entered into two supply contracts with local funeral directors for pubic hair harvested from embalmed corpses, and I hope that I can acquire enough pubic hair to keep my merkin business afloat while the strike lasts.

There is one little glitch, however. One of the directors conditioned acceptance of the contract on obtaining a favorable opinion letter from the California Board of Mortuary Science, to which he is now corresponding. I told him that I had run my proposal past my attorney who did not raise any problems with obtaining pubic hair from cadavers. This director insisted, however, that he had to obtain concurrence with your opinion from the Board of Mortuary Science. I only raise this to give you the "heads up" in case the Board contacts you about this.

Very truly yours,

J. Morgan Dumont

Keith L. Mason
Attorney

Pauline Copeland
Legal Assistant

Law Office of
Keith L. Mason, Inc.
Attorney at Law
██████████ *Street, Antioch, California 04500*

Telephone (925) █████
Facsimile (925) █████
E-mail: █████████.com
www.keithmason.com

March 7, 2010

J. Morgan Dumont, III
9663 Santa Monica Blvd.
Box 274
Beverly Hills, CA 90210-4303

Dear Mr. Dumont:

Okay. You got me, but you finally blew the gag by referring to the licensing agency as the "Board of Mortuary Science." When I tried to telephone it (rather frantically) in order to distance myself from you, I learned that no such board exists in California, and that the legitimate licensing agency for funeral directors is the "California Cemetery and Funeral Bureau".

I hope that I can someday discover your real name so that I can repay your kind attention. Until then, you'll be affectionately referred to in this office as the "Merkin Jerk".

Sincerely,

KEITH L. MASON
Attorney at Law

CHAPTER 12

Mr. Dumont and the Avian Slanderer

J. MORGAN DUMONT, III

9663 SANTA MONICA BLVD., BOX 274
BEVERLY HILLS, CALIFORNIA 90210-4303

January 6, 2010

CONFIDENTIAL

Martha L. Chambers, Esq.

████████████████████████

Woodland Hills, California 91367

Dear Ms. Chambers:

A mutual acquaintance has suggested that I contact you. I need the help of a trial lawyer. I realize that legal assistance for sophisticated litigation is not cheap, and I am prepared to pay an up front, non-refundable flat fee of $200,000 to the lawyer who I select. (I don't like paying lawyers by the hour because it encourages inefficiency and waste.) Although I realize that sophisticated litigation often costs more than $200,000, I thought that you might nevertheless be tempted to take my case if I paid a flat fee up front.

In order for you to assist me, you need some background information. I am a Managing Director of a prestigious investment bank and I am in charge of the company's real estate division. I come from a long line of financiers, and am independently wealthy as a result of inheritances. However, I have never allowed this to dilute my enthusiasm for hard work. I work an average of 82 hours per week, and I expect that that those who work under me do the same. I don't tolerate slackers. As far as I'm concerned, "sick days", "funerals", "wakes", and "family crises" are almost always euphemisms for "holidays". When you accept the king's ransom that I pay as a salary, I own you. It makes my blood boil to hear the principals and vice presidents under me whimper about working over 70 hours per week. My management style is admittedly tough. Confidentially, I believe that General Patton was right. Sometimes you have to slap people around in order to motivate them.

The litigation that I want to commence concerns a former principal in my company named Eric Johanson. At first, he worked hard (75-80 hours per week), and I thought that he had a future with my company. Thereafter, his effort fell to about 65 hours per week. In retrospect, he was a flash in the pan, and he lacked the work ethic to put in the extra effort that I require.

Of course, Johanson offered excuses for his less-than-stunning effort. (Slackers always have excuses). For example, his ten-year old daughter contracted a disease that caused her kidneys to fail temporarily. Johanson had a choice of either admitting his kid into the hospital or having her go on a dialysis machine as an outpatient for the six-month period of her treatment. I urged him to keep his kid in the hospital because I knew that he would miss work if he had to drive her to the dialysis treatments and stay there during the procedure. Notwithstanding my wishes, Johanson's daughter was placed on the outpatient dialysis program, allegedly because he wanted her to live a "normal life" during the six-month period when she had to be on a kidney machine. (I say "allegedly" because I have seen his daughter. She is so strange looking that she couldn't have a "normal life" if she wanted to.) In reality, Johanson wanted a break from the office, and his hours fell, just as I had predicted.

Next, Johanson's mother and father were involved in a car accident. The father died instantly. However, his mother's heart continued to beat even though she was brain dead. Of course, I sent Johanson a sympathy card. We were working on a large transaction at the time, and I couldn't afford for Johanson to be out of the office more than half a day, so I suggested to him that he hold a joint memorial service for his father and mother since the mother was as good as dead anyway. (Of course, I put the matter more tactfully to him). He refused, and just as I had feared, Johanson missed work for two funerals over the course of two weeks instead of just one. He nearly jeopardized a $113 million deal.

The last straw came while I was working on the acquisition of a large urban shopping mall. Johanson had a mild heart attack and was hospitalized for a week. Naturally, I was concerned, and I telephoned his cardiologist to find out about Johanson's condition. His physician said that, although Johanson did not need continual bed rest, he needed to "take things easy." I was entirely willing to accommodate Johanson, and I explained to him that, for the next three months, he only had to work between 8:00 a.m. and 6 p.m., and that he would have Sundays off entirely. The next day, Johanson telephoned me to say that he was quitting because he "couldn't take the pressure anymore." He said that, for the sake of his family, he had to get a stress free job. Johanson left me high and dry on the shopping mall deal, and, for reasons that are too complex to set forth here, the project ended up being less lucrative than it had at first promised to be. His irresponsibility enraged me.

About a year later, strange things began to happen. I started getting obscene phone calls one right after the other. These calls were obviously made by different men and each contained a solicitation for unnatural sex. Even though I was disgusted, I did not request an unlisted home telephone number since it is vital for business purposes that I remain accessible to clients and potential clients. However, my troubles did not stop with obscene phone calls. Soon, perverts started knocking on my door. In one month alone, five queers came prancing onto my property—some in broad daylight. Of course, I called the police, but they said that, unless they were soliciting sex for money, there were no laws that prohibited a homo from finding a partner.

Another odd thing happened, but this time at work. Someone left a figurine of a gray parrot on my desk with a note that said, "Ollie wants Morgan's organ." On my birthday, I walked into my office to see a pile of anonymous cards, all of which had pictures of parrots on them. Each card contained a gay oriented message. Obviously, disgruntled employees placed them there in order to humiliate me, although the significance of the parrot escaped me.

Two years after Johanson quit, I ran into an investment banker from a competing firm who was friends with Johanson. I asked him if he knew what Johanson was doing with his life. Johanson's friend told me that it had always been one of Johanson's dreams to be a veterinarian because he loved animals. Because Johanson had to support his family and could not go back to school to get a degree in veterinary medicine, he settled on purchasing a pet shop. (I always knew he was a nut case).

One day after work, I was in need of some laughs, and I asked my driver to pull up to Johanson's store. It was a few blocks from my usual route. I thought it would be amusing to see his new "enterprise". I walked into the store, but I did not see Johanson. I then went to the front counter. A gray parrot with red tipped wings stood on a perch that rested on the counter. A sign was placed under the perch that read:

HELLO, MY NAME IS OLLIE. I BITE. WATCH OUT.

As I walked up to the counter, the parrot screeched the following at ear-piercing volume: "Morgan Dumont dates men in the bathroom."   Store patrons actually laughed at this vulgarity. And then in two different voices, the bird said:

Voice # 1: Hello, I'm Ollie the parrot.

Voice # 2: Hello, I'm Morgan Dumont

Voice # 1: I bite, but Morgan sucks.

Then the bird blurted out the following in rapid succession: Call Morgan Dumont for good time!", and it shrieked out my telephone number, over and over again. I ran out of the store.

Of course, I put two and two together and realized that everyone at my firm knows about Ollie the parrot. I hired a private investigator to find out more. The investigator discovered that the only phrases that Johanson has taught him refer to me being receptive to homosexual acts. According to the investigator, the parrot insults me continuously every day with dozens of vulgar phrases. I also learned that my inferiors at the office frequent Johanson's store for sick entertainment, and, as a result, I have become the object of social ridicule.

To me, this is no laughing matter. At one time, I loved work, but now I can't wait for each day to end so that I can get out of the office and be out of sight and sound of constant sneers and jeers.

The first attorney that I consulted suggested that I could get a money judgment against Johanson for intentional infliction of emotional distress and possibly slander. I told this lawyer that getting a money judgment against Johanson wouldn't do me any good since my private investigator has told me that Johanson (to use the investigator's words) "doesn't have a pot to piss in." It's the continuing damage to my reputation that I'm concerned about, not money.

I want that bird DEAD.

Judges can order that dangerous dogs be destroyed, so why can't they execute this filthy bird that is destroying my life? I am prepared to pay the above-described fee and a bonus if my objectives are accomplished. I am interviewing one other lawyer, and I am asking both of you to give me your written preliminary thoughts as to how my objectives can best be accomplished as well as your brief analysis of the issues. I will review and compare your replies in determining which lawyer should be retained. Kindly correspond with me promptly.

Very truly yours,

J. Morgan Dumont, III

JMD/km

Law Offices of **Martha Chambers**

Woodland Hills, California 91367
TELEPHONE: (818) ▇▇▇▇▇
FACSIMILE: (818) ▇▇▇▇▇

January 26, 2010

J. Morgan Dumont, III
9663 Santa Monica Boulevard
Box 274
Beverly Hills, CA 90210

      Re: Dumont/Johanson

Dear Mr. Dumont:

    I am in receipt of your letter dated January 6, 2010, soliciting my assistance in a dispute you have with Mr. Johanson concerning his bird. I would be happy to take your case for $200,000 under the following circumstances:

    1. You will have to understand that the fee you pay me does not grant you any owner-ship in me or my services. For your money, you will get the best legal representation I can offer. That includes my best advice, which you may accept or reject. I will conduct myself within the bounds of the law and the ethical obligations incumbent upon attorneys. If you are looking for a puppet, or a shady operator, I am not the attorney for you.

    2. You do not control my time or the manner in which I conduct your case. You do control the litigation, and its objects, with one caveat: I WILL NOT ENDEAVOR TO HAVE THE BIRD KILLED. It has not harmed anyone physically, and it is not the bird's fault it was taught to repeat its defamatory communications. You are entitled to have the bird cease its de-famatory communications. That can be done by having the bird kept at Mr. Johanson's home, where its comments cannot be "communicated" to others. I will try to secure that result for you.

    3. I will take the $200,000 fee and place it in my trust account for allocation to my oper-ating account in the following manner: I will take a $20,000 non-refundable retainer to begin. I will transfer $5,000.00 a month from the trust fund to myself as fees. If the matter is resolved before I have transferred the full $200,000, I will transfer the remainder to myself at that time. If I have transferred the entire amount before the matter is resolved, you will owe me no more

fees. You will be billed for, and must pay independent of the fee, any costs incurred. If at any point in time we disagree about how this matter should be resolved, you will release me as your counsel of record. Any fees transferred to me up to that point will be mine, and you will owe me no more. I will return anything left to you.

If you wish to discuss this matter further, I would be happy to discuss it with you. I charge $500 for consultations.

Very truly yours,

LAW OFFICES OF MARTHA L. CHAMBERS

Great!!
Hire this Lawyer!!

J. MORGAN DUMONT, III

9663 SANTA MONICA BLVD., BOX 274
BEVERLY HILLS, CALIFORNIA 90210-4303

February 24, 2010

Martha L. Chambers, Esq.

Woodland Hills, California 91367

CONFIDENTIAL

Dear Ms. Chambers:

Thank you for your reply letter of January 26, 2010. I like your tough style.

As to point 1 of your letter, I agree. In the event I retain you, I won't "own" you. Actually, I'm not certain why you've gotten your pantyhose in a twist over this issue. After all, I want independent-thinking counsel, not a puppet.

You're unwilling to have that foul fowl destroyed. Okay. I accept that. However, your conclusion that everything will be fixed by having a court order Johanson to take that parrot home is not well considered. As was stated in my previous correspondence, my investigator says that Johanson invites people to his pet shop for sick entertainment. He holds drunken parties there while his perverted parrot insults me. If a court orders him to keep his parrot at home, Johanson will simply hold his depraved bacchanalias at his house instead. No doubt, he'll continue to invite queers to these gatherings, and his avian fagmonger will persist in drumming up interest among queers in having unnatural sex with me. This is no solution at all.

Therefore, I ask that you consider representing me in order to achieve a result that does not require the (well-deserved) execution of that winged vermin. I want that bird silenced. I've done extensive research on this issue, and I have discovered that researchers at Rutgers University have developed a specialized operation to "de-vocalize" noisy peacocks. Why can't a judge order that this operation be performed on this debauched, gutter-beaked pest? Wouldn't that result satisfy your humanitarian concerns? After all, what is more important? Aiding and abetting a slandering parrot or assisting me, a human being?

Very truly yours,

J. Morgan Dumont

J. Morgan Dumont

Law Offices of **Martha Chambers**

Woodland Hills, California 91367
TELEPHONE: (818) ████████
FACSIMILE: (818) ████████

March 1, 2010

J. Morgan Dumont, III
9663 Santa Monica Boulevard
Box 274
Beverly Hills, CA 90210

     Re: Dumont/Johanson

Dear Mr. Dumont:

I am in receipt of your letter dated February 24, 2010. 1 am confident we can think of a number of humane ways to address your legitimate concerns about the parrot. I don't know if mutilating the animal's voice box is the way to go, but certainly it is an option that can be evaluated, and even proffered as a bargaining tool to encourage Johanson to offer a less brutal and more satisfactory means of insuring your peace of mind. Similarly, there are many ways to deal with the unwanted attention you have been subjected to from other men.

I'm sure you realize that the story you tell does not paint you in a sympathetic light.: A jury might think you deserve the treatment you have received. However, I believe a Judge will be able to separate the situation that gave rise to Mr. Johanson's acts of ''revenge from the civil wrong his actions actually constitute. Please be advised however that there is always a risk that the Court would think this a situation where you should be a bit more ''thick skinned'' about all this, and relief could be denied entirely.

I am willing to try and secure a remedy for you. I am enclosing for your review and approval a retainer agreement that incorporates the terms set forth in my previous letter. If it is acceptable to you, please fax and mail the signature page to my office, along with the retainer fee.

Very truly yours,

Martha L. Chambers

Waltz & Grant Vechionne

Attorneys at Law PC

Pittsburgh, Pennsylvania 15219-1913

Phone: 412-█████ Fax:412-█████

Jill D. Grant
Direct Dial: 412-█████

February 2, 2010

VIA U.S. MAIL

J. Morgan Dumont, III
P.O. Box 266
Holicong, PA 18928-0266

Dear Mr. Dumont:

I write in response to your interesting, and somewhat troubling correspondence of January 29, 2010.

While I certainly mean no disrespect, if you do in fact need the services of an attorney in relation to the matters described, I hope that you can appreciate that the information recounted in your letter is, at best, rather unusual. As it is not my practice to simply ignore those who write to this office in search of legal assistance, I feel compelled to respond to your letter.

If your letter was written in jest, then perhaps I am too diligent or naïve or both.

However, if you are in need of legal services, please feel free to phone this office and we can discuss the matter further. I should advise you, however, that I do not take lightly defamatory comments concerning the race, religion, sexual orientation, or other immutable traits of any person or group of people, and I would appreciate your respecting that view and modulating your tone accordingly.

Very truly yours,

Jill D. Grant

Just playing hard to get

Follow up letter Required

J. MORGAN DUMONT, III

POST OFFICE BOX 266
HOLICONG, PENNSYLVANIA 18901

February 9, 2010

Jill Grant, Esq.
Waltz, Grant & Vechionne
█████████████████████
█████████████
Pittsburgh, Pennsylvania 15219███████

CONFIDENTIAL

Dear Ms. Grant:

Thank you for your reply letter of February 2, 2010. I can appreciate the fact that you find the circumstances in which I have found myself to be bizarre. However, I don't appreciate your apparent conclusion that this is some type of "jest." If this were happening to you, would you be laughing?

I trust, however, that you are still interested in taking my case. To that end, I'll drop in at your office on the way to work within the next two weeks.

In addition to the other issues that I addressed in my previous letter to you, I need to know whether I have the right under the law to self-help. I mean, suppose I break into Johanson's pet shop and terminate that slandering parrot with extreme prejudice. Will the law protect me under the circumstances? If not, is my liability for dispatching that filthy feathered thing significant enough to deter me from violating the law? I mean, how much can a parrot be worth anyway? The self-help option appeals to me even more than a court case. In light of the unusual facts of this controversy, wouldn't bringing this matter in a public forum invite publicity and thereby destroy my reputation everywhere? Please advise.

Very truly yours,

J. Morgan Dumont

J. Morgan Dumont

Waltz & Grant Vechionne
Attorneys at Law PC

Pittsburgh, Pennsylvania 15219-1913

Phone: 412-■■■■■ Fax:412-■■■■

Jill D. Grant
Direct Dial: 412-■■■■■

February 11, 2010

J. Morgan Dumont, III
P.O. Box 266
Holicong, PA 18928-0266

Re: Your Correspondence of February 9, 2010

Dear Mr. Dumont:

I write in response to your correspondence of February 9, 2010.

In regard to your inquiry concerning self-help, I remind you, firstly, that since we have not even met, no attorney-client relationship has been established and, therefore, I am not positioned at this time to offer you legal advice. However, as you appear to be aware, the self-help you propose includes a criminal violation of the law. I would never advise a client to break the law in order to resolve a dispute. Thus, if this is the sort of legal advice you are seeking, you might want to consider another attorney.

As for your suggestion that you will ''drop in'' at my office, I also should advise you that I see clients and potential clients only by appointment. My schedule is such that an unannounced visitor is likely to be disappointed, as I often have meetings and engagements scheduled, both in and out of the office and, so, your chances of finding me available for an unscheduled meeting are not good. If you would like to schedule an appointment, please phone my office and we can set up a mutually agreeable time for such a meeting.

Very truly yours,

Jill D. Grant

J. MORGAN DUMONT, III

POST OFFICE BOX 266
HOLICONG, PENNSYLVANIA 18901

March 8, 2010

CONFIDENTIAL

Jill Grant, Esq.
Waltz, Grant & Vechionne
████████████████████

████████████

Pittsburgh, Pennsylvania 15219-████

Dear Ms. Grant:

I received your letter advising me against adopting the "self-help" option in dispatching that filthy bird. In re-reading that letter, I eventually got the message between the lines. Of course, you're right. I shouldn't get directly involved, so I'll hire someone to do it for me. That way, no one can say that I engaged in illegal "self-help."

If for any reason my alternative means of resolving this matter does not soon effectuate the desired result, I'll make arrangements with you for a consultation.

Very truly yours,

J. Morgan Dumont

J. Morgan Dumont

NO REPLY!

The Law Offices of Paul M. Klaust
& Associates
15 N. Northwest Hwy.
Park Ridge IL 60068-3339
847-686-3111

January 19, 2010

J. Morgan Dumont, III
104 W. Chestnut Street, Box 219
Hinsdale IL 60521-3387

Dear Mr. Dumont:

I am in receipt of your letter of January 7, 2010. Although, for a number of reasons, I doubt its credibility and take it as a prank, on the remote chance that this is a sincere attempt to retain legal Counsel, I have a suggestion. Since the courts are already clogged with ridiculous lawsuits brought by people with great resources and a self-centered view of their rights, may I suggest an alternative to litigation. I suggest that you take half of the retainer you proposed, buy the parrot, and dispose of your property as you wish. I imagine that $100,000.00 might buy the whole pet store.

Frankly, I'm surprised that you would not have thought of this option on your own. Not being of a similar mind set as you, I must confess that I got this idea from the character "Mr. Potter" in that tribute to optimism and human nature, "It's A Wonderful Life." There is a scene where Mr. Potter tries to buy George Bailey so he can get rid of the thorn in his side, the Bailey building and loan. (Come to think of it, they, too, had a pet bird at the building and loan). I hope you have had a chuckle from this and I have given you the result you were looking for. If your letter was a serious attempt to secure counsel, like George Bailey, I have no desire to be "owned" by someone such as you and must respectfully decline your case.

Sincerely,

The Law Offices of Paul M. Klaust
& Associates

Paul M. Klaust
Attorney at Law

CHAPTER 13

Mr. Dumont's Constitutional Privacy Protection Invention

J. MORGAN DUMONT, III

9812 FALLS ROAD, SUITE 114, BOX 300
POTOMAC, MARYLAND 20854

January 5, 2010

Gordon D. Booth, Esq.
Davidson, Temple & Booth, P.C.
██████████████████
████████
Washington, D.C. 2001-████

CONFIDENTIAL

Dear Mr. Booth:

I need the help of a commercial lawyer with regard to a new product that I will be launching, and a mutual acquaintance recommended that I contact you. I realize that legal assistance for sophisticated commercial transactions is not cheap, and I am prepared to pay a non-refundable flat fee of $200,000 to the lawyer who I select for preparing the contracts and guiding me through the legal twists and turns of my new enterprise. (I don't like paying lawyers by the hour because it encourages inefficiency and waste.) Although I realize that legal counsel for sophisticated commercial matters often costs more than $200,000, I thought that you might nevertheless be tempted to take me on as a client if I paid a flat fee up front.

You need some background information in order for you to appreciate the legal issues that need to be resolved. Audio engineering is my vocation, and Civil War history is my avocation. A year ago, I read Shelby Foot's most recent Civil War book which largely dealt with General Sheridan's campaign in Virginia's Shenandoah Valley. I was struck by one account of a battle outside of Winchester, Virginia, where a rare acoustical phenomenon contributed to a Confederate defeat. The sound of gun and cannon fire was deafening from many miles away, but when a relieving column of rebel soldiers marched within a few miles of the battle, the guns suddenly became silent and only the sounds of nature could be heard. The relieving force of Confederates wrongly concluded that the battle had ended before their arrival, and they retreated.

In fact, the proximity of the Blue Ridge Mountains caused a phenomenon that eventually became known as an "acoustical shadow." Crudely stated, echoes cause acoustical shadows. As you know, sound travels in wavelengths. If the obstruction that produces the echo (e.g., the Blue Ridge Mountains) is at a precise distance from the listener who is standing at an oblique angle to both the obstruction and the sound's source, the wavelengths from both will reach the listener at the same time. However (and this is critical), the wave created by the echo will arrive at the listener's position off by one-half phase. The result: "Destructive interference", i.e., dead silence. This was the cause of the mysterious "acoustical shadow" experienced in the Civil War.

It occurred to me that, as a result of recent developments in audio pulse technology, it is now possible to create acoustical shadows anyplace at will. For example, a series of pulse audio devices can be planted in a room so that it is absolutely impossible to tape a conversation unless the speaker is within 8 inches of the surveillance microphone.

I won't bore you with the technical details, but you should know that my new device mimics the sound wave patterns caused by a speaker's voice but at sub and hypersonic wavelengths. These wave patterns are designed to reach all corners of the room at exactly one-half phase off the wavelengths that carry the speaker's voice. (Of course, if I used wavelengths audible to humans, no one could hear the speaker's words, which would defeat the usefulness of the invention.) Sub and hypersonic wavelengths work only because of an additional device that I created which replicates "white noise." White noise is equivalent to "white light" in the field of spectroscopy—-they contain all audible and visible wavelengths, respectively. As a result, if the room where a conversation takes place is bugged, the tape recorder at the other end will be able to record nothing but dead silence.

My invention has already been patented. My problem is how best to market it without getting the federal government (affectionately referred by me as BIG BROTHER) involved. I am concerned about BIG BROTHER because the target market for my product is, to be honest, people who wish to avoid surveillance. Although this could include company executives trying avert industrial sabotage or defense/national security personnel, the truth of the matter is, I'll make the biggest profits from this device by selling to Italians. If you don't believe me, ask John Gotti how much he would have paid for my invention.

If I sell my device as a prophylactic to industrial sabotage, BIG BROTHER will undoubtedly require merchants to sell it only to persons who have a license to own and operate surveillance equipment. The customers who will pay the most for my device are not likely to go to the authorities in order to obtain such a license. Alternatively, BIG BROTHER might outlaw the device in the same way that Virginia and Michigan have outlawed the sale and use of radar detectors. Also, I don't want BIG BROTHER claiming that I have somehow obstructed justice because some drug dealer whose home was bugged happened to benefit from my product.

I need a lawyer to get me through the maze of BIG BROTHER's statutes and regulations so that I can safely sell it to the Italians and maximize my profits. Can you help?

I am interviewing one other lawyer, and I am asking both of you to give me your written preliminary thoughts as to how my objectives can best be accomplished as well as your brief analysis of the issues. I will review and compare your replies in determining which lawyer should be retained. Kindly correspond with me promptly.

Very truly yours,

J. Morgan Dumont, III

**LAW OFFICE OF
GORDON D. BOOTH**

▮▮▮▮▮▮▮▮ AVENUE
SUITE ▮▮▮▮▮
WASHINGTON, D.C. 20014-▮▮▮

LICENSED IN
MARYLAND AND THE
DISTRICT OF COLUMBIA

MARY P. NEWCOME
OF COUNSEL
LICENSED IN MARYLAND

(301) ▮▮▮▮▮4

(301) ▮▮▮▮▮0

(301) ▮▮▮▮▮9
(FACSIMILE)

January 19, 2010

J. Morgan Dumont, III
9812 Falls Road
Suite 114
Box 300
Potomac, MD 20854

    Re: <u>Your letter of January 5, 2010</u>

Dear Mr. Dumont:

    I am writing in response to your letter which was received in my office (belatedly) on January 14, 2010. I am somewhat intrigued by your proposition, as well as by your new enterprise.

    As you may know, the Civil War is also my avocation, since I have visited virtually all of the local battlefields, as well as many of the important sites throughout the country. I guess one prime example of this avocation is the fact that I proposed to my wife on Henry Hill, at the site of the first battle of Manassas. As you may also know, I have in the past filed suits against Janet Reno and the Department of Justice, the Sheriff of Montgomery County, as well as the Prince George's County Department of Social Services, and other governmental departments and agencies.

    I found your approach interesting, and felt that it certainly warranted a response. However, I would deem it critical, as well as essential, that we meet in person to discuss what you expect and what you anticipate and what your demands upon your counsel would be. As you may know, I have a very active practice and am quite busy with my current caseload. Obviously, working with you may entail some curtailing of my existing practice, as well as rearranging certain administrative priorities for my office.

    I think I could provide able assistance to you on the topics you mentioned, and could also possibly help in more practical ways regarding marketing, direction and other approaches. I am not sure where you have heard of me, or where you obtained my name, but you probably know from whoever referred you that I do have certain clients who deal (at least peripherally) in the sound of audio engineering. At best, I am familiar with the concepts if not the science.

As stated above, I would like to meet with you to discuss matters relating to this situation and would be glad to meet with you at a convenient time and place, either here in D.C. or some other alternative location. I would not charge for any initial meeting or consultation regarding what I can do for you, and what you are looking for in the way of counsel.

If you are interested in a face-to-face meeting you may write to me at the above address or give me a call at the above phone numbers. You should note that I will be out of the office for one week from January 24 to January 28 for a much-needed vacation. I look forward to hearing from you in the future.

Sincerely,

Gordon S. Booth

Great!!
Hire this lawyer!!

J. MORGAN DUMONT, III

9812 FALLS ROAD, SUITE 114, BOX 300
POTOMAC, MARYLAND 20854

February 10, 2010

Gordon D. Booth, Esq.
Davidson Temple & Booth, P.C.
████████████████████
██████████

Washington, D.C. 20001████

CONFIDENTIAL

Dear Mr. Booth:

Thank you for your well-considered letter of January 19, 2010. I applaud your anti-government activities in support of personal liberties. With you at the helm, I'm sure that we'll find a way of getting around intrusive and competition-stifling state and federal laws. More than ever, I feel that my interferometer will be a great success and that someday, no Italian family in America will even think about sitting down for a bowl of spaghetti before turning on one of my devices.

However, I have one serious concern that needs to be addressed before I arrange a face-to-face meeting with you. I was intrigued by the fact that you, too, are a Civil War buff. On the other hand, when I read about your love of Civil War history and how you proposed to your wife on a battleground of a famous Confederate victory, I suddenly became concerned about your surname. I trust that you're not related to the infamous John Wilkes Booth. As much as I think you're the right man for the job, I don't want to be associated with persons who are even remotely responsible for Mr. Lincoln's assassination. Please advise.

Very truly yours,

J. Morgan Dumont

J. Morgan Dumont

LICENSED IN
MARYLAND AND THE
DISTRICT OF COLUMBIA

MARY P. NEWCOME
OF COUNSEL
LICENSED IN MARYLAND

**LAW OFFICE OF
GORDON D. BOOTH**

████████████████
4█████████████ AVENUE
SUITE ████████
WASHINGTON, D.C. 20014-████

(301) ████████4

(301) ████████0

(301) ████████9
(FACSIMILE)

February 17, 2010

J. Morgan Dumont, III
9812 Falls Road
Suite 114
Box 300
Potomac, MD 20854

     Re: <u>Your letter of February 10, 2010</u>

Dear J. Morgan Dumont:

    I am in receipt of your letter of February 10 and was somewhat amused by your concern about my relationship with John Wilkes Booth.

    Let me assure you that although the name is the same, I know where my family was at that time, and they were nowhere near the State of Maryland and we have no relationship whatsoever to "the Mad Booths of Maryland". I trust that puts you somewhat at ease.

    As I have suggested previously, I would recommend a face-to-face meeting so that we can meet and discuss matters relating to your situation and what I can do for you and what specifically you are seeking from your attorney.

Sincerely,

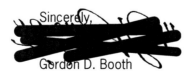

Gordon D. Booth

Paula de Cardona
Attorney at Law

███████████ *Street*
Northridge, CA 91325
Web: www.k██████.com

(818) ████████
Facsimile (818) ███████
E-mail: ██████████*@aol.com*

January 12, 2010

J. Morgan Dumont, III
9663 Santa Monica Blvd.,
Box 274
Beverly Hills, CA 90210-4303

Dear Mr. Dumont:

Thank you for contacting me regarding the marketing of your invention. I thought your letter was, at the very least, entertaining.

Unfortunately, preliminary thoughts on ways to reach your goals and a brief analysis of issues would still require me to invest a substantial amount of time without the certainty of being ultimately retained. You want far more than an estimate. You want me to provide you with legal strategies at no cost to you, in exchange for the mere hope that I will become the successful bidder.

I am sorry Mr. Dumont to disappoint you but you must pay a retainer up front if you want my legal thoughts and analysis. I estimate that a retainer of $5,000 would be sufficient for me to prepare the initial information you seek. If you conclude from my preliminary efforts that I should be retained for the remainder of the legal work to be performed, you can deduct the $5,000 from the non-refundable flat fee. If you conclude otherwise, then at least I will have been justly compensated for my legal work.

Just playing hard to get

Follow up letter Required

Very truly yours,

PAULA DE CARDONA

PDC/mm

J. MORGAN DUMONT, III

9663 SANTA MONICA BLVD., BOX 274
BEVERLY HILLS, CALIFORNIA 90210-4303

January 20, 2010

Paula de Cardona, Esq.

████████████████

Northridge, CA 91325

CONFIDENTIAL

Dear Ms. De Cardona:

I assure you that I had no intention of trying to dupe you into giving me free legal advice. Although I now see why someone could misconstrue my method of selecting legal counsel as an attempt to obtain free legal advice, I assure you that I had no intention of taking advantage of you or anyone else. To be candid, I am hurt that you think me capable of anything so sinister, and I suggest (in an avuncular way) that you should not automatically think the worst of people.

Far from trying to deny you your just emolument, I would like to augment your compensation by also paying you a commission on the sales of my interferometer. (I solicited your help in the first place because I deduced from your surname that you are of Italian heritage.) As I indicated in my previous letter, I've decided to target my sales efforts towards your kind since they have the most incentive to avoid government surveillance and would presumably be willing to pay top dollar for my invention.

I need to obtain customer lists of Italians, especially Sicilians. (When it comes to finding customers for my interferometer, the swarthier the better). Since (1) the Mafia is everywhere and (2) you are an Italian in the legal business, I naturally concluded that you might be some boss' consiglieri. I am prepared to give you a 15% commission on the sales price of any interferometer sold to a person to whom you have referred me. (I'll even give a 10% sales discount to members of your family). If you're interested, why don't you draft up a commission agreement for me to sign when I drop in at your office on February 8th. I look forward to meeting you.

Very truly yours,

J. Morgan Dumont

J. Morgan Dumont

Paula de Cardona
Attorney at Law

███████████ *Street*
Northridge, CA 91325
Web: www.█████*.com*

(818) ██████
Facsimile (818) ██████
E-mail: ██████*v@aol.com*

January 28, 2010

J. Morgan Dumont, III
9663 Santa Monica Blvd.,
Box 274
Beverly Hills, CA 90210-4303

Dear Mr. Dumont:

Show me a certified check made payable to me for $5,000.00 as a non-refundable retainer for my initial research, and I'll be happy to chat with you on February 8, 2010. Be warned, however, that I will not be able to give any legal advice at this "getting-to-know-you" introduction. If after we meet, you don't feel that I am the right lawyer for your project, you can put the $5,000.00 certified check back in your pocket and walk out the door with no obligation.

In the event that you wish to proceed after our initial meeting, I will take your check and prepare an analytical memorandum addressing the most important legal issues raised by your plan to market your interferometer. Once that research is concluded, then I will proceed with representing you in exchange for and additional $195,000.00 non-refundable flat fee, provided, however, that you sign a retainer agreement that specifically sets forth the scope of the work expected from me.

Believe it or not, Mr. Dumont, I don't know any mobsters. Sorry. Therefore, I will not be drafting any commission agreements with respect to the sale of your anti-surveillance device.

Very truly yours,

PAULA DE CARDONE

CHAPTER 14

Mr. Dumont's Stand Against an Airborne Assault

J. MORGAN DUMONT, III

104 W. CHESTNUT STREET, BOX 219
HINSDALE, ILLINOIS 60521-3387

January 5, 2010

Jason E. Logan, Esq.

████████████████

████████████

Chicago, Illinois 60601

CONFIDENTIAL

Dear Mr. Logan:

I need the help of a trial lawyer with respect to my son's victimization by a teenaged thug, and a mutual acquaintance recommended that I contact you. I realize that legal assistance for serious litigation is not cheap, and I am prepared to pay a nonrefundable flat fee of $100,000 to the lawyer who I select. (I don't like paying professionals by the hour because it encourages inefficiency and waste.) Nevertheless, I realize that sophisticated litigation often costs more than $100,000, but I thought that you might be tempted to take my case if I paid a flat fee up front.

My son, Tyler, is a 17-year old high school junior at our State's most exclusive prep academy. He is an outstanding student. Tyler is also the President of the Chess Club. Moreover, he is already an accomplished classical ballet dancer. Not only is Tyler academically oriented, but he has also demonstrated an entrepreneurial inclination. For example, he had the idea of persuading the owners of nurseries and flower shops to give him flower petals from wilting or old plants. He then processed and sold those free materials as expensive potpourri. Tyler is a refined lad, artistically inclined and sensitive. His mother and I are very proud of him.

The problem arose last spring when a member of the Academy's lacrosse team, Burt Polinski, took a dislike to Tyler and started to taunt him. (Polinski was no doubt accepted into the Academy because of his lacrosse skills, and I have heard (from good authority) that Polinski depends upon a financial need based grant). Polinski is clearly not representative of the Academy's enrollment, which is drawn almost exclusively from the cream of the crop.

Something disgusting happened one afternoon at the Academy following Tyler's participation in Dance Club. He had just finished showering and was dressing on a bench in the boy's locker room. Polinski had finished lacrosse practice and was undressing next to Tyler. As usual, Polinski promptly began to taunt Tyler and used vulgar language about him, but Tyler ignored his brutish behavior.

Apparently frustrated with Tyler's refusal to dignify his taunts, Polinski dropped his underwear, spread his buttocks and moved his hams next to Tyler's face. At the same time, Polinski said (and I quote), "Hey Tyler, tell me if my farts smell like your potpourri?" Then the animal flatulated in my son's face. Tyler was traumatized by this degradation, and he has not been himself since. As a result of this event, we have had to increase Tyler's visits to his psychiatrist from three to five times per week.

I met with the Headmaster as soon as I heard about this outrage. To my shock, the Headmaster decided to punish the animal by restricting his after school activities for one week only. That added insult to injury.

I've subsequently met with the local prosecutor for the purpose of commencing a criminal action against the animal. The prosecutor refused to do so, explaining that it was in his discretion to decline to represent Tyler with respect to such "minor" (believe it or not) disturbances of the peace. However, he explained that I had the right to retain a lawyer who would act as a private prosecutor. Consequently, I promptly canvassed my contacts in the legal community about whether they would take the case.

Unfortunately, I now realize that I have asked the wrong type of lawyer to take the case. My contacts with the legal community revolve around the world of mergers and acquisitions. It was a shock to me that these attorneys simply had no enthusiasm for the case. (However, to be fair to them, they probably thought I wanted to saddle them with a freebee since my company's legal costs exceed $3,000,000 annually.)

Each of these lawyers told me that the case would not hold up as either an assault or battery in either a civil or criminal proceeding. They corresponded with me, explaining that an assault is defined as the act of "placing a victim in immediate apprehension of harmful or offensive contact." They concluded that, because Tyler had not believed that the animal would actually flatulate in his face, the animal could not have "assaulted" Tyler as a matter of law. As I understand it, this is because Tyler never "immediately apprehended" the animal's offensive contact.

In addition, these lawyers told me that a battery action would not be successful because the legal definition of battery (if my notes are correct) is the act of actually "making harmful or offensive contact with the person of another." These commercial lawyers insisted that no battery took place because the animal only flatulated and did not make any harmful or offensive contact with Tyler. <u>However, Tyler is prepared to testify that he had felt a wisp of hot, moist air against his cheek at the time of the animal's attack.</u> Doesn't this satisfy the "offensive contact" test?

This has become a top priority for me. Even though I understand that Polinski's battery might not constitute an indictable offense, I am looking for a lawyer who is willing to pull out all the stops for my boy. In other words, I want to sue Polinski and (if possible) his parents in a civil proceeding, criminal prosecution or both.

I am interviewing one other lawyer, and I am asking both of you to give me your written preliminary thoughts as to what litigation strategy you would employ as well as your brief analysis of the issues. I will review and compare your replies in determining which lawyer should be retained. Kindly correspond with me promptly.

Very truly yours,

J. Morgan Dumont

J. Morgan Dumont, III

JMD/km

Jason E. Logan
ATTORNEY AT LAW
█████████ Drive
Suite ████
Chicago, Ill 60601
(312) ████████
Fax: (312) ███████

January 12, 2010

J. Morgan Dumont, III
104 W. Chestnut Street, Box 219
Hinsdale, Illinois 60521-3387

Re: Contemplated lawsuit against Burt Polinski

I am receipt of your letter dated January 5, 2010. While I am willing to meet with your son and you to discuss the contemplated lawsuit against Mr. Polinski, I am unwilling to delineate my litigation strategy in writing. My reason for this unwillingness has no reflection on the merits on your son's case. Rather, it is based on a prior situation in which I received a similar request. In that instance, I spent considerable time delineating in writing my trial strategy. I subsequently found out that the prospective client hired another attorney and used my work to litigate the action.

If you and your son are still serious about pursuing this litigation, I would appreciate it if you would promptly call me at the above number to arrange a mutually convenient time to meet and discuss the contemplated suit. I await your call.

Very truly yours,

Jason E. Logan

Interview Required
Drop In !!

J. MORGAN DUMONT, III

104 W. CHESTNUT STREET, BOX 219
HINSDALE, ILLINOIS 60521-3387

January 26, 2010

Jason E. Logan, Esq.

███████████████

█████████████

Chicago, Illinois 60601

CONFIDENTIAL

Dear Mr. Logan:

Thank you for your reply letter of January 12, 2010. You're absolutely right. Let's meet. I have to be in Chicago on Thursday, February 10, 2010, for a business appointment in the afternoon. Unless it is inconvenient for you, I'll plan to come in with Tyler at 10:00 am. That should give us plenty of time to talk.

As you know, I've asked one other lawyer to look at the facts, but when I read in your letter that you already had a "prior situation in which you received a similar request," I immediately concluded that you're probably the best man for our flatulence assault case.

I look forward to hearing about your trial strategy in the other flatulence assault case that you reviewed. Perhaps the same strategy that you mapped out there can be used to bring Polinski to justice.

By the way, do you think that I'm correct that offensive contact required in civil assault cases did, in fact, occur when Tyler felt the breath of bowel against his cheek? Just curious.

I'm anxious to meet you.

Very truly yours,

J. Morgan Dumont

J. Morgan Dumont

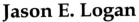

Jason E. Logan

ATTORNEY AT LAW

████████ Drive

Suite ████

Chicago, Ill 60601

(312) ████████

Fax: (312) ████████

February 1, 2010

Dear Mr. Dumont:

I am in receipt of your letter dated January 26, 2010. I would be willing to meet with Tyler and you at 11:00 a.m. on February 10, 2010, since I will be in court at 10:00 a.m. Please call me and advise whether that time is convenient.

Very truly yours,

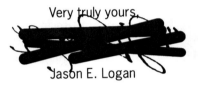

Jason E. Logan

J. MORGAN DUMONT, III

104 W. CHESTNUT STREET, BOX 219
HINSDALE, ILLINOIS 60521-3387

February 7, 2010

Jason E. Logan, Esq.

████████████

████████████

Chicago, Illinois 60601

CONFIDENTIAL

Dear Mr. Logan:

You completely failed to respond to my request for information corroborating your boast to me that that you have had similar flatulence assault experience. Your inability to provide me with that information evidences the fact that you have puffed up your "flatulence assault" credentials in order to get your hands on the $100,000 fee. I need a lawyer with solid experience in this area of law, not some shyster blowing more hot air.

Very truly yours,

J. Morgan Dumont

J. Morgan Dumont

NO REPLY!

LEONARD D. FURST, JR., P.A.

TRIAL LAWYERS BUILDING
633 S.E. THIRD AVENUE, SUITE 302
FORT LAUDERDALE, FL 33301
(954) 764-4849; FAX (954) 764-4731

DAN S. ARNOLD III
  TRIAL LAWYER

January 10, 2010

J. Morgan Dumont, III
6901 W. Okeechobee Boulevard, D-5
Box 161
West Palm Beach, Florida 33411

Re: Tyler Dumont

Dear Mr. Dumont:

I received your letter today regarding your son's situation. This unfortunate matter presents interesting legal issues. You are correct in your assessment that this would be a complicated case, particularly if we expect to achieve any meaningful results. However, it is not my practice to provide legal analysis before actually speaking with a potential client. Therefore, before I do anything, I need to speak with you and probably your son. Please call upon receipt of this letter so that we can further discuss this matter and my potential involvement.

Sincerely,

Leonard D. Furst, Jr.
For the Firm

Great!!
Hire this Lawyer!!

J. MORGAN DUMONT, III

6901 W. OKEECHOBEE BLVD., D-5, BOX 161
WEST PALM BEACH, FLORIDA 33411

January 26, 2010

CONFIDENTIAL

Leonard D. Furst, Jr., Esq.
██████████████████████████
████████, Suite ████████
Fort Lauderdale, Florida 33301

Dear Mr. Furst:

   Thank you for your reply letter of January 10, 2010. Finally, I have found a lawyer who understands the severity of Tyler's injury and who stands willing to redress a profound degradation of another human being. I think you're right. Let's meet. My schedule is fairly unpredictable, but it looks like I can meet with on Thursday, February 10, 2010, at 10:00 A.M. Unless this date is inconvenient for you, I'll see you then.

   About your suggestion to interview Tyler, I think that this is an excellent idea. Ever since Polinski's assault, Tyler has been almost entirely uncommunicative. For hours each day, he sits on his bed, reliving the attack, rocking back in forth in a state of self-induced catatonia. I will plan to bring Tyler's psychiatrist to the meeting in the event that he has one of these spells during your interview. The psychiatrist is the only person who can snap Tyler out of these spells.

   I look forward to meeting you.

Very truly yours,

J. Morgan Dumont

J. Morgan Dumont

Leonard D. Furst, Jr., P.A.

Trial Lawyers Building
633 S.E. Third Avenue, Suite 302
Fort Lauderdale, FL 33301
(954) 764-4849; Fax (954) 764-4731

Dan S. Arnold III
   Trial Lawyer

February 1, 2010

J. Morgan Dumont, III
6901 W. Okeechobee Boulevard, D-5
Box 161
West Palm Beach, Florida 33411

Re: Proposed February 10, 2010 meeting

Dear Mr. Dumont:

    I have received your letter of January 26 and your proposal to come to my office on February 10 for an interview. I am sorry, but I will be out of the office that day on a prior commitment and will not be able to accommodate you. Please telephone me to set a mutually convenient date for me to meet with you, Tyler and his psychiatrist.

    I was distressed to read the description of your son's injury. I am terribly sorry for his suffering. In this regard, it would be helpful when we meet for you and Tyler to authorize his psychiatrist to discuss his medical condition, symptoms and prognosis with me. If we are to obtain a judgment for substantial damages, I am afraid that your son's psychiatric problems will have to be presented to the court in an open proceeding. Of course, whatever information you, Tyler or his psychiatrist discloses to me now will be held strictly confidential until such time when Tyler and you expressly authorize its disclosure in a court of law.

Sincerely,

Leonard D. Furst, Jr.
For the Firm

J. MORGAN DUMONT, III

6901 W. OKEECHOBEE BLVD., D-5, BOX 161
WEST PALM BEACH, FLORIDA 33411

February 9, 2010

Leonard D. Furst, Jr., Esq.
█████████████████████████
██████ , Suite ██████
Fort Lauderdale, Florida 33301

CONFIDENTIAL

Dear Mr. Furst:

I have received your reply correspondence of February 1, 2010. Thank you. Tyler's psychiatrist has informed me that he cannot meet at your office. However, he is available to meet with us at his office on any Monday, Tuesday or Thursday after 6:00 p.m. between February 15 and 28. I hope that this is acceptable to you. Since I am trying to coordinate this meeting, I will need a series of dates when you can meet with Tyler, me and his psychiatrist.

The other lawyer with whom I have corresponded about Tyler's case turned out to be a phony who exaggerated his qualifications in order to get my money. Unless something unanticipated occurs, it looks as if we will be cementing our lawyer-client relationship when we meet. Accordingly, I will bring a certified check to our meeting to cover the $100,000 non-refundable flat fee.

Tyler remains despondent, frequently unable to snap himself out of his compulsion to relive Polinski's flatulence assault. We try to do everything possible to keep Tyler's mind from dwelling on that terrible day, but if he is in the presence of anyone who breaks wind, he starts convulsing. Sometimes, fetid odors will stimulate a full-blown seizure with uncontrollable salivation and loss of bowel and bladder control. It is therefore essential that no one pass gas in Tyler's presence.

To that end, I have taken the liberty of enclosing 6 Gas-Ex® tablets for you to begin taking 48 hours before our meeting with Tyler. Also, please refrain from eating the following gas-producing foods at least 36 hours before our appointment: Asparagus, broccoli, brussel sprouts, cabbage, cauliflower, corn, cucumbers, garlic, leeks, onion, peas, peppers, radishes, sauerkraut, turnips, carbonated soft drinks, sugar substitutes, baked beans, chickpeas, lima beans, kidney beans, apricots, cantaloupes, prunes, raw apples and dairy products (if you are lactose intolerant). It is ESSENTIAL that you take the Gas Ex® tablets and avoid the above-referenced foods in order to ensure that Tyler does not have a seizure during our appointment.

Thank you. I look forward to receiving from you the list of dates on which you are available to meet.

Very truly yours,

J. Morgan Dumont

J. Morgan Dumont

NO REPLY!

CHAPTER 15

Mr. Dumont's Knee Slapper

J. MORGAN DUMONT, III

POST OFFICE BOX 266
HOLICONG, PENNSYLVANIA 18901

Herbert J. Kalb, Esq.

January 4, 2010

Champaign, Illinois 61824-

CONFIDENTIAL

Dear Mr. Kalb:

I need the help of a trial lawyer, and a mutual acquaintance has suggested that I contact you. I realize that the services of a good litigator are not cheap, and I am prepared to pay an upfront, non-refundable flat fee of $200,000 to the lawyer who I select. (I don't like paying lawyers by the hour because it encourages inefficiency and waste.) Although I realize that sophisticated litigation often costs more than $200,000, I thought that you might nevertheless be tempted to take my case if I paid a flat fee up front.

In order for you to help, I need to give you some personal information about me. I am the great grandson of a famous financier, and our family is one of the richest in America. The need to work for a living clouds people's judgment about life, but being born rich gives one a clearer perspective. When every material desire can be satisfied simply by ringing for a servant, the deception created by ambition, work and struggle is stripped from you. Don't misunderstand me. I'm not denigrating those who must work for a living. I am simply stating that, if you aren't burdened with work, you can see life and its significance through a clearer lens and observe an undistorted reality. What is that reality? It is simply this--life itself is meaningless and we are all destined for oblivion.

As a youth, I was pre-occupied with death and dying. Obviously, everything is condemned to dust and the soul (if it exists) is ultimately consigned to the blackest of voids. Nothing has meaning when measured against the depth of the grave. As a result of these insights, I lived a nearly humorless life, and what little levity I found came from appreciating life's absurdity. I found it ironic that people place so much importance on their labors which, in reality, have no more significance than the toiling of ants.

One day, it hit me. Life's absurdity is precisely what makes living bearable! Think about it. Life is miserable because we take ourselves too seriously and fail to appreciate the profound irony (and humor) from the fact that mankind is cosmically irrelevant. People need to see the humor of life, especially at its darkest moments. In order to survive, we need to be able to laugh at ourselves when things are at their worst. I think that this attitude should be fostered in our society, and I decided to do something about it by starting a business (albeit a part-time one) selling humorous sympathy cards.

I advertised for clients for my humorous sympathy cards, offering custom verse to suit specific situations. It took me several months to get my first commission. At last, I got a call from a man who read my advertisement. His best friend's wife had died. The husband of the deceased (i.e., the caller's friend) blamed himself for not taking his wife's health complaints seriously because she had been a hypochondriac. As it turned out, there wasn't anything that the husband could have done for her anyway. In reality, his wife died from liver disease resulting from years of alcoholism. The man who commissioned me wanted to help the husband get over his irrational guilt. Accordingly, I composed the following sympathy card:

You thought she was a faker
When you tried to awake her.
Hypochondria it wasn't.
Does it matter? It doesn't.
That she's dead is certain,
And we must draw the curtain.
'Twas love of drink that killed her.
'Twas booz, not blood, that filled her.
A sinner--her death, our loss.
Her vice? Quaffing the sauce.
Alas, she died, not from neurosis,
But from a bad case of liver cirrhosis.

Immediately after I sent the card to husband of the dead alcoholic, I got another commission. I guess that in the humorous sympathy card business, just like in any other, "when it rains, it pours." At the time, I was dating a home duty nurse who was taking care of a terminally ill ballet instructor named Timothy. When Timothy died, his family was devastated, and I convinced his nurse that a humorous sympathy card might be just the thing to catapult the family out of its grief. I therefore composed and sent to the following sympathy card to Timothy's family:

> I pen this verse
> While watching his hearse
> And hugging his nurse,
> So let be terse.
> We all knew he was gay
> From his dainty sashay.
> All thought he had AIDS
> E'vn his nurse and his maids.
> It shocked us to hear
> (And we all shed a tear)
> That Timmy, the dancer
> --a gay blade prancer--
> Died of plain old cancer.

Within the last three weeks, I have received telephone calls from two lawyers. Both attorneys said that they represented the immediate families of the deceased and that they were going to sue me for sending the above-quoted sympathy cards. Both lawyers demanded huge sums of money as a settlement, warning that unless I paid, I would be sued for intentional infliction of emotional distress. This seems frivolous to me. Don't they see that I was just trying to lighten things up? Besides, is the First Amendment dead in this state?

I am prepared to pay the above-referenced fee to the attorney that I select. More than just money is at stake for me. It's the principle of the thing. I am interviewing one other lawyer, and I am asking both of you to give me your written preliminary thoughts as to how my objectives can best be accomplished as well as your brief analysis of the issues. I will review and compare your replies in determining which lawyer should be retained. Kindly correspond with me promptly.

Very truly yours,

J. Morgan Dumont, III

JMD/km

Law Office Of Herbert J. Kalb, Ltd.

P.O. ████ I██████████████████
Champaign, Illnois 61824-0468 4████████████████
Phone: 217.█████
Fax: 217.█████

Herbert J. Kalb
Principal

Josef E. Poore
Associate

12 January 2010

J. Morgan Dumont, III
104 W. Chestnut, Box 219
Hinsdale, IL 60521–3387

Re: Intentional Infliction of Emotional Distress

Dear Mr. Dumont:

I have read your letter of 5 January 2010, including your proposal for retaining counsel to defend your interests in the two claims asserted against you for intentional infliction of emotional distress. I understand and respect your initial reaction to these claims, i.e., that they seem frivolous. However, unfortunately, the law has evolved to the point that these claims could be pursued through the Court system, and perhaps presented to a jury. If and when such a claim was presented to a jury, I am sure you understand the possibility of a runaway jury finding liability and assessing ridiculous damages. Again unfortunately, our legal system does not provide sufficient protection form the arbitrary actions of runaway juries.

This is not to say that the law does not provide some guidelines to be followed by competent judges and responsible juries.

Consider the fact that anyone can file a lawsuit these days. The facts that you describe are sufficient for an aggressive and creative lawyer to file suit and pursue pretrial discovery, including compelling sworn deposition testimony from you. Although the initial allegations of suit could be attacked by motion, the allegations would probably be sufficient to initiate discovery procedures. The attorneys could easily allege (though perhaps not prove) the essential elements for the claim of intentional infliction, to wit: that your conduct was truly extreme and outrageous; that you knew there was at least a high probability that your conduct would cause severe emotional distress; and that your conduct did, in fact cause severe emotional distress.

As to the first and second elements, a judge or jury might well view your conduct as outrageous under the circumstances, especially where you were aware that the claimant was particularly susceptible to emotional distress because of the recent death of a loved one.

Perhaps your best defense would focus on the third requirement, that the claimant did indeed suffer "severe emotional distress." Unfortunately, we do not know the extent or degree of emotional distress suffered or even alleged. Thus, it would be important for your attorney to thoroughly investigate this issue by subpoenaing medical, psychological, counseling and therapy records, and taking the sworn testimony of the claimant 'in deposition.

You might also be helped by a line of cases that holds that "severe" emotional distress is determined by considering its intensity and duration, and a single outrageous act is usually insufficient to support such a claim.

As an aside, your letter made reference to your rights under the First Amendment, Unfortunately, the First Amendment only restricts the government from infringing on its citizens' free speech. Private citizens are not restricted by the First Amendment, which allows a number of different legal actions based on unacceptable speech, i.e., libel, slander, intentional infliction of emotional distress, etc.

I would, of course, represent you on the terms proposed in your letter, a non-refundable flat fee of $200,000. (I agree that hourly fees contribute to inefficiency and waste in the legal industry.) I would bill separately for all court costs and litigation expenses. Depending on the venue of the lawsuit and location of witnesses, travel expense could be a significant component of your litigation costs.

I look forward to hearing from you.

Very truly yours,

Herbert J. Kalb

Great!! Hire this lawyer!!

J. MORGAN DUMONT, III

104 W. CHESTNUT STREET, BOX 219
HINSDALE, ILLINOIS 60521-3387

January 28, 2010

Herbert J. Kalb, Esq.

▉▉▉▉▉▉▉▉▉▉▉

▉▉▉▉▉▉▉▉▉▉▉▉▉

Champaign, Illinois 61824▉▉▉▉▉▉

CONFIDENTIAL

Dear Mr. Kalb:

Thank you for your thoughtful responsive letter of January 12, 2010. Your perspective on the humorous sympathy card business gave me a lot to think about.

I liked the first paragraph of your letter the best, in which you stated that you "understand and respect [my] initial reaction to these claims, i.e., that they seem frivolous." Exposing these claims as frivolous should be the focus of our defense. What do you think? If you agree with me, I think that it would be appropriate for us to meet. Please write back with times and dates for an appointment. In addition to the $200,000 check for the non-refundable flat fee, is there any documentation that I should bring to our meeting?

By the way, the client who commissioned my first humorous sympathy card (about the hypochondriac/alcoholic dead wife) hasn't yet paid me for my service. Do you handle collection cases, too? For all the aggravation that I've received, I should at least be paid. Please advise.

Very truly yours,

J. Morgan Dumont

J. Morgan Dumont

Law Office Of Herbert J. Kalb, Ltd.

P.O. ⬛
Champaign, Illnois 61824-0468
Phone: 217.⬛
Fax: 217.⬛

Herbert J. Kalb
Principal

Josef E. Poore
Associate

9 February 2010

J. Morgan Dumont, III
104 W. Chestnut, Box 219
Hinsdale, IL 60521-3387

Re: Intentional Infliction of Emotional Distress

Dear Mr. Dumont:

In response to your letter of January 28, I am available to discuss your case with you at any time in the afternoon on the following dates: February 15, 16, 18. Please telephone my office as soon as you receive this letter to schedule an appointment. In addition to the retainer check, please bring to our meeting copies of your sympathy cards, contracts, or any other correspondence that relate in any way to the persons claiming to be emotionally distressed by your writing.

The strategy of treating the claimants' cases as frivolous might indeed be worthwhile pursuing, but at this juncture, I am not in a position to commit to any particular strategy or tactic before getting all the facts and researching the relevant law. You should know, however, that I will pursue any strategy within the bounds of the law that will achieve your exoneration.

Lastly, I think that you ought not to try to collect your fee for authoring the card send to the husband of the alcoholic wife. In the event that the husband sues your client, your collection efforts will undoubtedly provoke him into filing a counterclaim against you for indemnification or contribution. In short, in the event that complaints are in fact filed against you, we should concentrate one hundred percent of our effort on getting them dismissed.

I hope the foregoing answers your questions. I look forward to meeting you.

Yours very truly,

Herbert J. Kalb

HJK/ma

J. MORGAN DUMONT, III

104 W. CHESTNUT STREET, BOX 219
HINSDALE, ILLINOIS 60521-3387

February 15, 2010

Herbert J. Kalb, Esq.

██████████████

██████████████

Champaign, Illinois 61824-████

CONFIDENTIAL

Dear Mr. Kalb:

I have decided to give the $200,000 non-refundable flat fee to another lawyer who has the guts both to defend me and collect the unpaid fees for my cards to which I am entitled. You seem to forget that this is my business. I don't write humorous sympathy cards for free.

Although I've decided that I need to retain a lawyer with more fortitude, I am grateful for your well-considered thoughts about my case. I would like to repay you in a way that might prove to be mutually profitable. In the event that you know anyone who is in the market for a humorous sympathy card, please give them my name and address. If they retain me, I'll kick back to you 15% of the contract price as your commission. Please let me know if you're interested.

NO REPLY!

Very truly yours,

J. Morgan Dumont

J. Morgan Dumont

JMD/km

William T. Harper, P.A.
Attorney at Law

January 10, 2010

J. Morgan Dumont, III
6901 W. Okeechobee Blvd., D-5
Box 161
West Palm Beach, Florida 33411

RE: REPRESENTATION ON 1ST AMENTMENT CLAIM

Dear Mr. Dumont:

Thank you for considering my firm to represent you in your probable lawsuit involving a claim of tortious conduct; namely, that the card you sent, on behalf of a client, did cause harm as a result of your intentional infliction of emotional distress.

Please understand that I do not provide any analysis of issues and render legal opinions until I am first retained. I would be happy to meet with you in person to discuss your case so we can evaluate the facts and the ability of each to work together. It is difficult to do so through the mail and a letter.

The most important aspect of an attorney-client relationship is trust and candor.

From only that contained in your letter, I will candidly tell you this: If you wrote that letter at the request of a client and sent it, then it is the client's communication and the client should be held responsible for its content. If you suggested that it should be sent and you sent it on as your own communication to the family, you can be held directly liable. If the client asked you to send it, then I would consider impleading the client(s) as a third party. That way if you are held liable at all, then you have a claim against the third party.

As an approach, I would strongly recommend—through counsel—calling the other side and apologizing in writing if it offended them.

████████ **Boulevard • Jacksonville, Florida 32207 • 904-**████ **• Fax 904-**████
e-mail: ████ **aol.com**

I would look at any avenue to work this out. The reason is that the humorous sympathy approach, while I understand the approach and purpose, is somewhat shocking. There will be many jurors outraged by this card and not find it funny shortly after someone has passed away. Thus, the question is who should be held accountable? If you did this on your own, you will have a tough road ahead, even in light of the First Amendment. The reason is as follows: commercial speech is treated differently than pure, political speech and receives less protection.

I hope that helps. If you would like to arrange a meeting, please call me at (904) ████.

Again, thank you for considering me and I remain,

Yours truly,

William T. Harper

Great!!
Hire this lawyer!!

J. MORGAN DUMONT, III

6901 W. OKEECHOBEE BLVD., D-5, BOX 161
WEST PALM BEACH, FLORIDA 33411

January 28, 2010

William T. Harper, Esq.
▬▬▬▬▬▬▬▬▬▬▬
Jacksonville, Florida 32207

CONFIDENTIAL

Dear Mr. Harper:

Thank you for your thoughtful responsive letter of January 10, 2010. You don't pull any punches. I like that. You've given me a lot to think about, too.

I think it's time for us to meet. I'll be in Jacksonville on Monday, February 14, 2010, for a morning business appointment. Unless it is inconvenient for you, I'll plan to drop in around 2:00 p.m.

Initially after receiving threats to sue, I concluded that my humorous sympathy card idea was too far ahead of its time. However, I was gratified (and felt somewhat vindicated) by your statement that you understand the "approach and purpose" of my humorous sympathy card service. Now, on further reflection, I think that there must be more enlightened people like you and me who can appreciate a service that can cause even the bereaved to laugh.

In short, your letter got me to thinking. Maybe I should insist that my clients sign indemnity contracts whereby they promise to pay for any damages (including legal fees) in the event some hyper-sensitive recipient is offended by one of my cards. To that end, in addition to the contemplated trial work, would you be able to draft a solid indemnity agreement?

I think that it's important to continue my work, not just because it serves the public interest, but also because it might look like an admission of guilt if I suddenly stop my humorous sympathy card service immediately after being sued. What do you think?

In any event, I look forward to meeting you.

Very truly yours,

J. Morgan Dumont

J. Morgan Dumont

William T. Harper, P.A.
Attorney at Law

February 7, 2010

J. Morgan Dumont, III
6901 W. Okeechobee Blvd., D-5
Box 161
West Palm Beach, Florida 33411

Dear J. Morgan Dumont:

Your letter of January 28 concerns me. You do not seem to realize how much trouble you are in. In my opinion, you and I should spend our time and efforts on heading off what might prove to be a very serious lawsuit against you for intentional infliction of emotional distress. Now is certainly not the time to focus on finding a way for you to insulate yourself from liability with respect to humorous sympathy cards that might be authored by you in the future.

As I stated in my last letter to you, you need to meet with me in order to fashion a strategy to prevent litigation and/or to devise a legal defense in the event that a complaint is actually served upon you. I indicated that it would be worthwhile for us to reach out to the complainant's counsel and possibly apologize in writing. This should be the subject of our meeting. Please telephone me immediately for a time and date that is convenient for you to meet. To repeat, I believe that it is urgent that you take such action now.

Yours truly,

William T. Harper

Boulevard • Jacksonville, Florida 32207 • 904-████ • Fax 904-████
e-mail:████aol.com

J. MORGAN DUMONT, III

6901 W. OKEECHOBEE BLVD., D-5, BOX 161
WEST PALM BEACH, FLORIDA 33411

February 15, 2010

William T. Harper, Esq.
██████████████████
Jacksonville, Florida 32207

CONFIDENTIAL

Dear Mr. Harper:

I read your letter of February 7, 2010, admonishing me to keep my eye on the ball and focus on resolving the current dispute first before worrying about future contacts for my humorous sympathy cards. After reflecting on your letter, I now see the wisdom of your advice, and I'll try never again to put the proverbial "cart before the horse."

In order to stave off a lawsuit by apologizing, I have taken your advice and have mailed the following written explanation to the hypersensitive husband who received a humorous sympathy card about his dead, drunken wife:

Dear Mr. Cassall:

I am the author of the humorous sympathy card that Mr. Caldwell sent to you after your wife's death. My lawyer, William T. Harper, Esq., suggested that I write this letter of apology to you since you have evidently taken umbrage to my sympathy card.

I sincerely regret that you have misinterpreted the sentiments expressed in that card as being intended to cause you emotional injury. I assure you that I had no such intention. Far from it. I only wanted to jolt you out of your grief by causing you to laugh.

Please allow me to explain. I understand from Mr. Caldwell that you are an intelligent man. As a smart person, you no doubt have abandoned fairytale beliefs about the existence of god or life after death. As you must realize, your wife, like the rest of us, was nothing but a collection of atoms no more significant than any other. Only by recognizing the meaninglessness of life and our absurd preoccupation in finding any purpose in it can we laugh when life seems its darkest.   This was on my mind when I composed my humorous sympathy card that Mr. Caldwell sent to you.

Maybe your wife might never have become an alcoholic if she had been able to cope with the fact of her ultimate worthlessness. It's been quipped around town that she tried so hard to find meaning in a bottle that her own blood was 80 proof! Well, no matter. We're all destined to decay. In that regard, perhaps your wife is more special in death than she was in life. After all, it's been said that we're all just food for worms, but in her case, she's the food and the drink! Hoping that you got a chuckle from this now knowing the spirit in which it is written, I remain, Yours truly...

Hopefully, your instruction that I should apologize in writing will assuage his anger and end his plan to sue me.

I need your input with regard to the written apology to the parents of the gay dancer who died of cancer. I understand that his parents are decidedly unintelligent and won't be able to grasp the ironic humor of taking their meaningless lives so seriously. In short, they won't be able to understand the point behind humorous sympathy cards. I'm not exactly sure what to say to them, especially since everything I wrote in the card about their queer son was true. Can you help?

Please write to me with dates and times when we can meet in order to discuss our strategy to head off a lawsuit from the dancer's family. Thank you.

Very truly yours,

J. Morgan Dumont

JMD/km

William T. Harper, P.A.
Attorney at Law

February 18, 2010

Certified Mail, # Z 328 757 150
J. Morgan Dumont, III
6901 W. Okeechobee Blvd., D-5
Box 161
West Palm Beach, Florida 33411

Dear J. Morgan Dumont:

I am responding to your letter of February 15 which I received today. As you know, I have not been retained by you, and I am not your lawyer. Therefore, you had no right to represent to the bereaved widower that I am your attorney, much less suggest to him that I had approved the contents of your written "apology" to him.

Instead of retaining me after a consultation, you unilaterally took action, mailing a written "apology" that was as outrageous as the first card that you sent that got you into trouble. By implicating me as a participant in the mailing of your last correspondence, you have made me your potential co-defendant in a lawsuit for intentional infliction of emotional distress. Unfortunately, my defense must be that you acted without my knowledge, much less consent. Because I will be forced to point the blame towards you, it would be a conflict of interest for me to represent you, and I must decline your request for representation.

In the event that I am impleaded into your lawsuit as a result of your false representation to the husband of the deceased, I expect you to do the honorable thing and admit that you acted on your own without my knowledge or consent. In the meantime, you must do two things. First, find a different lawyer to represent you now. Second, DO NOT WRITE ANY MORE LETTERS.

Yours truly,

William T. Harper

Boulevard • Jacksonville, Florida 32207 • 904- • Fax 904-
e-mail: aol.com

O'TOOL & PIERSON, L.L.C., P.C.
ATTORNEYS AT LAW
███████ STREET
PHILADELPHIA, PENNSYLVANIA 19107

James J. O'Tool
Orville P. Nicholas*

*Also Member of NJ Bar

215-███████
215-██████ FAX

████████ Drive
Voorhers, NJ 08043
(609)██████

February 11, 2010

J. MORGAN DUMONT, III
POST OFFICE BOX 266
HOLIGONG, PA 18929-0266

Re: Professional Services

Dear Mr. Dumont, III,

Mr. Pierson and I reviewed your missive of 29 January, 2010. My position and a brief analysis of the issues are as follows:

1. The heir to a fortune he was born
Of common tasks and toils he did scorn.
While riches gave his life perspective perspicuous
He obsessed with the morbid and ridiculous.

2. He grew to appreciate life's absurdity
And this helped shake his youthful lethargy.
He sought to ease grief with the humorous,
And it became a business, not mere hubris.

3. Suddenly the gay dancer passed away.
His skill as a bard he would display.
The grieving family reacted with displeasure.
They hired, not one, but a second lawyer for good measure.

4. The defendant offered counsel a fixed retainer,
But this would soon be exhausted and leave a remainder
And though $200,000.00 was offered by the troubled jester,
To the skilled counsel who penned these words, it is but a token gesture.

Best of luck with other counsel,

JAMES J. O'TOOL

JJO/pw

About the Author

KENNETH L. MCELWEE, a Phi Beta Kappa scholar from the College of Wooster, attended Vanderbilt University School of Law, where he was the Associate Editor of the Vanderbilt journal of Transnational Law. After receiving his Juris Doctorate, Mr. McElwee served as a law clerk to The Honorable Frederick B. Lacey, a federal district judge who sat the Foreign Intelligence Surveillance Court and Temporary Emergency Court of Appeals. As a trial lawyer, Mr. McElwee became a partner of one of New Jersey's largest law firms where he practiced commercial litigation and represented dozens of "Fortune 500" companies. At the age of 38, he retired from the practice of law.

Breinigsville, PA USA
28 November 2010
250227BV00004B/1-108/P